W0471675

Vorwort

Liebe Schülerinnen und Schüler, liebe Eltern,

herzlich willkommen zu einem ganz besonderen Übungsband für das Fach Englisch in der 9. Klasse am bayerischen Gymnasium! Seit der Einführung **LehrplanPLUS** hat sich der Englischunterricht grundlegend verändert: Er ist praxisnäher, lebendiger und orientiert sich noch stärker an den Anforderungen der modernen Welt.

Schulaufgaben von bayerischen Gymnasien

Englisch 9

Was dieses Buch einzigartig macht: **Die Aufgaben basieren auf tatsächlich gestellten Original-Schulproben von Nachhilfeschülern unseres Durchblicker Lernstudio Arndt!** Das bedeutet, ihr übt mit echten Prüfungsaufgaben, die direkt aus dem Schulalltag bayerischer Gymnasien stammen – authentischer geht es nicht. Unsere erfahrenen Lehrerinnen und Lehrer haben diese Aufgaben sorgfältig ausgewählt, ergänzt und an den aktuellen LehrplanPLUS angepasst. So seid ihr optimal auf die Herausforderungen der 9. Klasse vorbereitet.

In diesem Band findet ihr sieben komplette Schulaufgaben mit ausführlichen Lösungen. Die Aufgaben decken alle wichtigen Kompetenzbereiche ab:

Vocabulary (Wortschatz)

Grammar (Grammatik)

Speaking (Sprechen)

Translation (Übersetzung)

Text Production (Texterstellung)

Reading Comprehension (Leseverstehen)

Listening Comprehension (Hörverstehen)

Alle Aufgaben entsprechen dem aktuellen Niveau der bayerischen Gymnasien und sind ideal abgestimmt auf die Lehrwerke

Green Line 5 und Access 9

und erfüllen somit voll den **LehrplanPLUS**. Durch regelmäßiges Üben mit diesen Schulaufgaben wirst du sicherer, selbstbewusster und kannst deine Noten gezielt verbessern. Sollte es einmal nicht auf Anhieb klappen, findest du in den Lösungen hilfreiche Erklärungen und Tipps, um gezielt an deinen Schwächen zu arbeiten.

Mein Ziel ist es, deine Motivation und Kreativität beim Englischlernen zu wecken und dich Schritt für Schritt zum Erfolg zu führen. Mit Ausdauer, Spaß und einem klaren Plan wirst du die nächste Schulaufgabe meistern – und vielleicht sogar richtig Freude an der englischen Sprache entwickeln!

Ich wünsche dir viel Erfolg und vor allem viel Freude beim Lösen der Aufgaben!

Deine Englischtrainerin

Monika Arndt

Monika Arndt (Dipl.-Übersetzerin), veröffentlichte als Buchautorin Ernährungsbücher für Kinder in den Verlagen dtv und Ravensburger. **Das Baby-Kochbuch**, **Wie Kinder fit und gesund bleiben** und **Das Ravensburger Kochbuch für Kinder** mit Bildern von Ali Mitgutsch.
Zuvor hat Monika Arndt in verschiedenen Redaktionen gearbeitet, z.B. über zehn Jahre in der Redaktion des Schulfernsehheftes beim Bayerischen Schulfernsehen. Beim Stark-Verlag hat sie über Produktion und Inhalt von Lernhilfen Erfahrungen gesammelt, geeignete Lehrer gesucht und die Bücher als Lektorin redigiert.
Sie unterrichtet Englisch und Französisch im ***Durchblicker Lernstudio Arndt***.

Titelbild: Heinrich Schmid, Überlingen am Ried / Singen am Hohentwiel
Alle Fotos, die abgebildet sind, stammen von unsplash.com
www.durchblicker.org

Die **Listening Comprehensions** (Schulaufgabe 1.1, Schulaufgabe 2.1, Schulaufgabe 2.2 und Schulaufgabe 3.2) finden Sie in der Lösung und sind dem Schüler vorzulesen. Alternativ finden Sie auf unserer Homepage www.durchblicker.org unter Bayern Englisch 9 die entsprechenden Audio-Dateien zum Abspielen. Der QR-Code führt Sie direkt zu den Audio-Dateien.

ISBN **978-3-946141-64-8**

9 783946 141648

Inhaltsverzeichnis

1. Schulaufgabe aus dem Englischen (1.1)
I. Listening Comprehension (sehr anspruchsvoll)
Demographics and ethnic groups in Australia
II. Vocabulary
Fill in the gaps with the correct words from unit 1
III. English Language Proficiency / Grammar
a) Decide whether you need the Future progressive or Future perfect in the following sentences and fill in the gaps accordingly
b) Decide whether you need the dynamic or stative form of the verbs
IV. Text Production
Australia's prime minister Scott Morrison decided to be tougher on immigrants. He thinks that Australia does not need more immigrants but less. He argues that immigration is not beneficial for Australia. Recently he has decided that new migrants have to wait four years before they can access government welfare payments. Write a formal letter to Scott Morrison and tell him what you think of his new position regarding migrants

1. Schulaufgabe aus dem Englischen (1.2)
I. Reading Comprehension
Travel tips every first time Sydney visitor needs to know – Things to know the day you land
a) Assign each paragraph a heading from below. NOTE: There are two extra headings which you do not need
b) Answer the following questions in short sentences
c) Decide whether the following statement is true (T), false (F) or not in the text (NT)
II. Vocabulary
Explain the following words from unit 1 in your own words (resident, victim, refugee, desperate, wealthy)
III. Translation
Translate these sentences into English
IV. English Language Proficiency / Grammar
Spot 20 mistakes in a text. Underline and correct them

1. Schulaufgabe aus dem Englischen (1.3)
I. Reading Comprehension
Read this text carefully and answer the questions
Study: the Fridays for Future movement is facing ist limits
a) Decide which of the following statements is true (T), false (F) or not in the text (NT)
b) Answer the following questions. Try to use your own words
II. English Language Proficiency / Grammar
Spot 2 mistakes in each sentence and correct them
III. Translation Translate the following sentences into English. Pay particular attention to vocabulary from unit 1 & 2

2. Schulaufgabe aus dem Englischen (2.1)
I. Reading Comprehension
Read this text carefully and answer the questions
How sustainable are ‚eco' brand high street fashions?
There's a new trend among popular fashion brands: „eco friendly" collections. Organic cotton is everywhere this summer, but is the label just a marketing strategy?
a) Answer the questions
b) Multiple Answer: Tick the correct answers for each question
c) Decide which of the following statements is true or false

II. English Language Proficiency / Grammar
a) Rewrite the following sentences by using a participle construction
b) Find synonyms or antonyms for five words
III. Text Production
The article presented in this exam's reading comprehension provided you with a lot of information on the problem concerning fast fashion and sustainability. Now imagine the following: To make fashion more sustainable, the parliament of Ruritania has just decided that from now on every piece of clothes will cost twice the amount it costs now.
A pair of sweat pants, for example, now cost 40€ instead of 20€. Do you think that is a good idea? Make a clear argument on either yes or no

2. Schulaufgabe aus dem Englischen (2.2)
I. Listening Comprehension (leichteres listening)
Listen to a text about the first humans in Australia. You will hear the text twice. Decide whether the following statements are true (T), false (F) or not in the text (NT)
II. Vocabulary
1. Translate the words from unit 2
2. Fill in the gaps with vocabulary from unit 2&3. Mind grammar and tenses where necessary
III. English Language Proficiency / Grammar
1. Change the following sentences into indirect speech
2. Rewrite each sentence with a participle construction
3. Answer the following questions with *So, Neither, Nor*

3. Schulaufgabe aus dem Englischen (3.1)
I. Reading Comprehension Read the following text carefully and answer the questions below
Gender: Early Socialization
Gender socialization is the process through which children learn about the social expectations, attitudes and behaviours typically associated with boys and girls. This topic looks at this socialization process and the factors that influence gender development in children
Decide which of the following statements is true (T), false (F) or not in the text (NT)
II. Vocabulary
Fill in the gaps with words from unit 3
III. English Language Proficiency / Grammar
Put the following words in the correct order to form a sentence. Pay attention to punctuation
IV. Translation
Translate the following excerpt from the reading comprehension into German

3. Schulaufgabe aus dem Englischen (3.2)
I. Listening Comprehension
Listen to a text about how to write a CV (curriculum vitae). You will hear the text twice
10 steps to a successful CV (curriculum vitae)
a) Decide which of the following statements is true (T), false (F) or not in the text (NT)
b) Answer each question *briefly* (sometimes one or two words are enough)
II. English Language Proficiency / Grammar
Stressing sentence parts: Alan is planning a holiday in the USA. He's at a travel agency. Answer the questions in full sentences. Use five different ways of stressing the answers
III. Text Production
Write a short cover letter / personal statement for the internship advertisement. Apply what you have learned in unit 3. As this job is fictional, you may invent skills but make sure your statement fits the proposed position

1. Schulaufgabe aus dem Englischen

Name: ____________________________

Stoff: Unit 1

I. Listening Comprehension *(Text aus Lösung 2x vorlesen lassen oder Audio in Durchblicker.org hören)*

Demographics and ethnic groups in Australia

Listen to a text about demographics and ethnic groups in Australia. You will hear the text twice. Decide whether the following statements are true (T), false (F) or not in the text (NT). Do not panic if there is a word you do not know / understand. Just keep listening and focus on the questions at hand

Vocabulary you might not know to boast: rühmen; thereby allocating

1. Australia is densely[1] populated.

O T O F O NT

2. Australia was fully colonized by the British Empire in the 18th century.

O T O F O NT

3. More than half of the indigenous population of Australia died during the era of colonization.

O T O F O NT

4. Many immigrants hoped to find work in Australia in the mid-1800s.

O T O F O NT

5. By the late 1800s, many Germans went to Australia.

O T O F O NT

6. Shortly after the beginning of the 20th century, no German passed the immigration test.

O T O F O NT

7. After World War II, only a few people from Europe and Asia decided to make Australia their new home.

O T O F O NT

8. About 5 million Australians are of Chinese descent today.

O T O F O NT

9. Australia's immigration policy is one of the best in the world.

O T O F O NT

---

[1] densely: dicht

10. Not everyone in Australia is happy with the state's immigration policy.

O T   O F   O NT

____/10

II. Vocabulary

The following definitions / descriptions have been taken from the famous "Oxford Learner's Dictionaries". Fill in the gaps with the correct words from unit 1

1. not fit to live in; impossible to live in: ________________
2. being the only one of its kind: ________________
3. a period of unusually hot weather: ____________________
4. a person who has been attacked, injured or killed as the result of a crime, a disease, an accident, etc.: __________________
5. a person who has been forced to leave their country or home, because there is a war or for political, religious or social reasons: _____________________
6. large or important enough to have an effect or to be noticed: _______________________
7. that is legally or officially acceptable: ________________
8. to become greater in amount, number, value, etc.; to make something greater in amount, number, value, etc.: ______________________
9. the top layer[2] of the earth in which plants, trees, etc. grow: ___________________
10. a duty to deal with or take care of somebody / something, so that you may be blamed if something goes wrong: ____________________

____/10

III. English Language Proficiency / Grammar

a) Decide whether you need the Future progressive or the Future perfect in the following sentences and fill in the gaps accordingly

Tanya hopes that by the time she finishes her last exams, she ________________________ (earn) enough money in her part-time job to travel to Sydney. She is sure that she _____________________ (have) a good time there. She ______________________ (spend) two weeks in the city. Tanya hopes that she _______________________ (improve) her English skills by the time she arrives in Sydney. If not, she ________________________ (struggle) with understanding the people there. Tanya __________________________ (stay) in a very cheap hostel in Sydney and she ___________________________ (not have) a room for

[2] layer: Ebene, Schicht, Lage

herself. Fortunately, her best friend ____________________________ (travel) with her, so she won't be all alone. However, her friend ____________________________ (not save) enough money by the time they arrive in Australia, either. Perhaps they ____________________________ (chose) a different city, because Sydney is not cheap.

____/10

b) Decide whether you need the dynamic or stative form of the verbs below

1. I ___________________(have) an apple for breakfast.
2. This parfum _________________ (smell) nice!
3. I think you should _________________(see) your mother.
4. I ___________________ (feel) I should take a break.
5. He ___________________ (hate) his new girlfriend.
6. My boyfriend ______________________ (always lose) his wallet.
7. I ______________________(often see) my neighbour at the supermarket.
8. I ____________________(prefer) black.
9. My father ______________________(need) my help with something.
10. I _____________________ (agree) with him.

____/10

IV. Text Production

Australia's prime minister Scott Morrison decided to be tougher on immigrants. He thinks that Australia does not need more immigrants but less. He argues that immigration is not beneficial for Australia. Recently he has decided that new migrants have to wait four years before they can access government welfare payments.
Write a FORMAL letter to Scott Morrison and tell him what you think of his new position regarding migrants. Write NO LESS than 120 words

____

____

____

____

____

____

____

____

____/15

Total points ____/55

Lösung: 1. Schulaufgabe aus dem Englischen

I. Listening Comprehension *(Text aus Lösung 2x vorlesen lassen oder Audio in Durchblicker.org hören)*

Demographics and ethnic groups in Australia

Listen to a text about demographics and ethnic groups in Australia. You will hear the text twice. Decide whether the following statements are true (T), false (F) or not in the text (NT). Do not panic if there is a word you do not know / understand. Just keep listening and focus on the questions at hand

Australia
Demographics and ethnic Groups of Australia [short pause]
Australia is home to around 24 million people. The country is vast, with large tracts of uninhabited land. Nearly 90% of the people live in urban areas, which gives it a low population density. The population here is one of the most ethnically diverse in the world.

History of Colonization [short pause]
Australia was once a land of only the aboriginals or the indigenous people. Before the British colonization in 1788, over 500 different indigenous groups controlled the area. Each had their language, culture, and belief system. These individuals witnessed the changing of their home due to the arrival of European immigrants.
Records indicate that Dutch explorers were the first to come to the continent, but it was the British who decided to colonize the land towards the end of the 1700s. The first colony was established as a place for exiled prisoners from other parts of the world. Continued immigration forced the native inhabitants out of their territories. The era was filled with conflict and disease that led to the loss of nearly 60% of the indigenous population. Eventually, the country was separated into six colonies.
In the mid-1800s, settlers discovered gold. The hope for employment and financial gain brought thousands of more immigrants from other parts of Europe as well as China and India. By the late 1800s, the majority of the people who were born in Australia were of British or Irish descent.

History of Immigration [short pause]
After the colonies were united as one federation, the government enacted an Immigration Restriction Act. The goal of this policy was to restrict immigration to Europeans only. This period is sometimes referred to as the starting point for the White Australia Policy (an unofficial term). The immigration test required that immigrants seeking Australian residency write a dictated statement that was presented to them in any European language. This system worked to prohibit the entrance of thousands of migrants; after 1909, nobody passed the exam.
Post World War II, the Australian government encouraged immigration to the country. This movement provided a home for many displaced post-war refugees. Immigrants did not, however, only come from Europe during these 15 years. Many Asian immigrants took the opportunity to make Australia their home as well. From 1945 to 1960, 1.6 million people arrived.

Ethnic Diversity today [short pause]
Understanding the history of colonization and immigration in Australia helps to understand the current makeup of ethnic backgrounds found today. British continue to be the majority with 67.4% of the population. This is followed by other European ethnicities: Irish (8.7%), Italian (3.8%), and German (3.7%). Those of Chinese ethnicity represent 3.6% of the population and the Aboriginal, and Native Australians are now only 3%. Other ethnicities can also be found, though in smaller numbers: Indian (1.7%), Greek (1.6%), Dutch (1.2%), and Other (5.3%). The "Other" ethnicity includes individuals from many countries, particularly European and Asian.

Effects on Society [short pause]
Today, immigration policy in Australia celebrates multiculturalism and promotes residency status among people of varying ethnic backgrounds. The country now celebrates its differences and boasts its cultural diversity (over 200 languages spoken). In recent years, few social problems have occurred as a result of this diversity except for non-English speaking immigrants who have a difficult time finding high-level, skilled jobs. Some Australians have spoken out against increased immigration levels, however, especially from Asian countries. The government has responded by adopting multicultural policies and has also recognized the disadvantage and structural violence established against the native populations thereby allocating more funds for social programs to benefit the group.

[This article has been taken from World Atlas; July 18, 2019; https://www.worldatlas.com/articles/ethnic-background-of-australians.html]

1. Australia is densely populated.

○ T ✔ F ○ NT

Tipps & Tricks: *large tracts of uninhabited land* → Das Gegenteil ist also der Fall.

2. Australia was fully colonized by the British Empire in the 18th century.

✔ T ○ F ○ NT

Tipps & Tricks: 1788 = *mid/late 18th century*

3. More than half of the indigenous population of Australia died during the era of colonization.

✔ T ○ F ○ NT

4. Many immigrants hoped to find work in Australia in the mid-1800s.

✔ T ○ F ○ NT

Tipps & Tricks: *hope for work* → *work* ist ein anderes Wort für *employment.*

5. By the late 1800s, many Germans went to Australia.

○ T ○ F ✔ NT

Tipps & Tricks: Zwar steht im Text, dass in den frühen Jahren der Kolonisierung auch Menschen von Europa nach Australien gezogen sind, Deutsche werden hierbei aber nicht explizit erwähnt.

6. Shortly after the beginning of the 20th century, no German passed the immigration test.

✔T ○ F ○ NT

Tipps & Tricks: Da die Rede von *nobody* ist, schließt das alle mit ein, also auch Deutsche.

7. After World War II, only a few people from Europe and Asia decided to make Australia their new home.

○ T ✔F ○ NT

Tipps & Tricks: Im Text ist die Rede von 1,6 Millionen, somit also nicht *a few*.

8. About 5 million Australians are of Chinese descent today.

○ T ✔ F ○ NT

Tipps & Tricks: Chinesen machen lediglich 3,6% der Gesamtbevölkerung aus. Bei einer Gesamtbevölkerung von 24 Millionen Menschen, sind das also deutlich weniger als 5 Millionen.

9. Australia's immigration policy is one of the best in the world.

○ T ○ F ✔NT

Tipps & Tricks: Dies ist Ansichtssache. Im Text wird darauf nicht Bezug genommen.

10. Not everyone in Australia is happy with the state's immigration policy.

✔T ○ F ○ NT

Tipps & Tricks: *Some Australians have spoken out against increased immigration levels.*

II. Vocabulary

The following definitions / descriptions have been taken from the famous "Oxford Learner's Dictionaries". Fill in the gaps with the correct words from unit 1

1. not fit to live in; impossible to live in: *uninhabitable*
Tipps & Tricks: Antonym: *inhabitable*
2. being the only one of its kind: *unique*
3. a period of unusually hot weather: *heat-wave*
Tipps & Tricks: Antonym: *cold-wave*
4. a person who has been attacked, injured or killed as the result of a crime, a disease, an accident, etc.: *victim*
5. a person who has been forced to leave their country or home, because there is a war or for political, religious or social reasons: *refugee*
6. large or important enough to have an effect or to be noticed: *significant*
Tipps & Tricks: Synonyme: *(very) important, noteworthy*
7. that is legally or officially acceptable: *valid*
Tipps & Tricks: Antonym: *invalid*

8. to become greater in amount, number, value, etc.; to make something greater in amount, number, value, etc.: *(to) increase*

Tipps & Tricks: Antonym: *(to) decrease*

9. the top layer of the earth in which plants, trees, etc. grow: *soil*

10. a duty to deal with or take care of somebody / something, so that you may be blamed if something goes wrong: *responsibility*

Tipps & Tricks: Adjektiv: *responsible*

III. English Language Proficiency / Grammar

a) Decide whether you need the Future progressive or the Future perfect in the following sentences and fill in the gaps accordingly

Tanya hopes that by the time she finishes her last exams, she *will have earned* (earn) enough money in her part-time job to travel to Sydney. She is sure that she *will be having* (have) a good time there. She *will be spending* (spend) two weeks in the city. Tanya hopes that she *will have improved* (improve) her English skills by the time she arrives in Sydney. If not, she *will be struggling* (struggle) with understanding the people there. Tanya *will be staying* (stay) in a very cheap hostel in Sydney and she *will not / won't be having* (not have) a room for herself. Fortunately, her best friend *will be travelling* (travel) with her, so she won't be all alone. However, her friend *will not / won't have saved* (not save) enough money by the time they arrive in Australia, either. Perhaps they *should have chosen* (chose) a different city, because Sydney is not cheap.

Tipps & Tricks
Future progressive: Beschreibt eine Aktion / Handlung in der Zukunft die definitiv (bzw. äußerst wahrscheinlich) passieren wird. → *will/will not + be + Verb_ing*
Future perfect: Beschreibt eine Aktion / Handlung, die schon vor einem bestimmten Zeitpunkt in der Zukunft passiert sein wird. → *will/will not + have + Verb_past participle*
Im ***Future perfect*** darf anstelle von *will* auch *might* stehen, wenn eine Vermutung ausgedrückt wird, oder *should* bei einer Erwartung (siehe letzte Lücke im Text).

b) Decide whether you need the dynamic or stative form of the verbs below

1. I *am having* (have) an apple for breakfast.
2. This parfum *smells* (smell) nice!
3. I think you should *see* (see) your mother.
4. I *feel* (feel) I should take a break.
5. He *hates* (hate) his new girlfriend.
6. My boyfriend *is always losing* (always lose) his wallet.
7. I *often see* (often see) my neighbour at the supermarket.
8. I *prefer* (prefer) black.
9. My father *needs* (need) my help with something.
10. I *agree* (agree) with him.

Tipps & Tricks
Nicht jedes Verb kann in einer progressiven Form (ing-Form) verwendet werden. Verben, die bestimmte Aktionen **(dynamische Verben)** ausdrücken, werden oft in progressiver Form ausgedrückt. Folgende Verben werden MEISTENS nicht in progressiver Form ausgedrückt: *agree, be, like, hate, hear, imagine, know, need, prefer, promise, realize, remember, see.*
Beispiel: Satz 8: *I prefer black.* → Ich bevorzuge schwarz. Dies wird wohl auch in 5 Minuten noch der Fall sein 😉.
Die **progressive Form** kann bei anderen Verben (siehe Satz 6) hingegen auch dann verwendet werden, obwohl das Signalwort (hier: *always*) ja eigentlich immer die einfache Form anweist, da es sich ja um eine gewohnte Tätigkeit / Handlung handelt. Dies geschieht bei Dingen / Handlungen, die unerwartet passieren oder nicht geplant sind. Der Sprecher drückt hier ein Gefühl aus, z.B. ein nicht sichtbares Kopfschütteln wie bei Satz 6.

IV. Text Production

Australia's prime minister Scott Morrison decided to be tougher on immigrants. He thinks that Australia does not need more immigrants but less. He argues that immigration is not beneficial for Australia. Recently he has decided that new migrants have to wait four years before they can access government welfare payments.
Write a FORMAL letter to Scott Morrison and tell him what you think of his new position regarding migrants. Write NO LESS than 120 words

Dear Prime Minister Morrison,
my name is Max Mustermann, and I am from Germany. I am concerned with your new position on immigrants. Most migrants who came to Australia for a better life have made your country a better place. Australia today would not be as successful economically if it were not for all the immigrants in the past. Australia has always been a country of immigration. Your ancestors emigrated to Australia as well, please do not forget that. I think that your new plan to restrict government welfare payments for new migrants is wrong. It could alienate many highly skilled foreign workers. Australia has always benefitted from its openness. I hope you reconsider your position.
Kind Regards,
Max Mustermann

Tipps & Tricks
In einem **formalen Brief** (egal ob handschriftlich oder elektronisch) sollte immer auf die **korrekte Anrede** geachtet werden. *Dear Prime Minister* würde auch ausreichen. Da Scott Morrison dich nicht kennt, solltest du dich gleich im ersten Satz kurz vorstellen, so dass er weiß, mit wem er es zu tun hat. Minimum ist wie hier: Name und Wohnort / Land. Zusätzlich kannst du auch noch dein Alter oder deinen Beruf nennen, wenn du möchtest. Versuche Umgangssprache zu vermeiden und dein Schreiben höflich zu halten, völlig egal welche Position du vertrittst. Vermeide unnötig lange Sätze (da sich in diesen auch mehr Fehler einschleichen können). Wenn du ein bestimmtes Wort verwenden willst, aber nicht weißt wie es im Englischen heißt, versuche es zu umschreiben. Beispiel: Vorfahren: Ihre 'Vorfahren' sind auch nach Australien ausgewandert – *Your 'ancestors' emigrated to Australia as well* → *Many decades ago, your family also .....* oder *Most people in Australia are immigrants as their families have emigrated to Australia a long time ago and so did yours.*

1. Schulaufgabe aus dem Englischen

Name: ______________________________

Stoff: Unit 1

I. Reading Comprehension

Read the following text carefully and answer the questions below. It is advised to read through the questions first. Pay attention to the footnotes as there might be some words you do not know

Sydney

Travel tips every first time Sydney visitor needs to know – Things to know the day you land

1. ______________________________________

No, not the gemstone[3] (although you can find plenty of stores hawking shinies[4] when shopping in Newtown) – our public transport system's integrated payment method is called an Opal Card, and you can use it on ferries, trains, buses and the Light Rail. Remember to tap on and off[5] everywhere, otherwise you'll be charged the highest possible amount for your trip. Opal Cards have maximum daily and weekly charges, and you can load them with funds at train stations, convenience stores, and, if you're registered, online. But if you've got a packed wallet, you can actually scrap the Opal for all but buses, and use your bank card instead (you won't get any discounts, though).

2. ______________________________________

Sydney is one of Australia's biggest cities, but by most international standards it is a fairly compact place. Much of the city centre (the Central Business District, otherwise known as the

[3] gemstone: Edelstein
[4] hawking shinies: verhökernde Glitzersteine
[5] to tap on and off: zum Ein- und Ausschalten, hier: entwerten

CBD) and the trendy surrounding suburbs are easily explored by foot, and in fact, one of the best ways to familiarise yourself with the lay of the land is by taking a wander through Sydney's streets and parks. You can even cross the famous Sydney Harbour Bridge by foot, and be sure to check out Luna Park by Milsons Point if you do. If you're a seasoned walker in search of a more challenging trek[6], there are also many wonderful inner-city bushwalks and coastal paths to discover on Sydney's fringes[7].

3. ___________________________________

There are people who catch a ferry across Sydney Harbour to work every day. It's a legitimate form of public transport, and can be the fastest way to get from one part of Sydney to another. But it's also ridiculously scenic like a postcard. We've found some of the most stellar ferry trips[8]: you'll be sailing on the old chuggers[9] to Manly, down the river to Parramatta and out to Watsons Bay.

4. ___________________________________

Public transport in Sydney has a chequered past[10]; from our inexplicably scrapped tram network[11] to the one-way monorail that once encircled the CBD, some pretty questionable choices have marked this city's transit history. Trains and buses are prone to[12] delays and whole services can be suspended in bad weather. Ferries are gorgeous and run to a tighter schedule, but aren't that frequent either. Basically, Sydney does not have a fast, reliable, easy to use mass transit system, at least not yet. An extensive light rail extension is making certain parts of the city more navigable, and upgrades to Sydney Central Train Station are aiming to streamline the customer experience[13] and keep services slick[14]. There's no denying, by international standards, this city is a beautiful basket case. So, you might as well embrace it: plan ahead and enjoy the (long) journey.

5. ___________________________________

Ever tried a flat white? How about avocado on toast? We invented those (kind of). Here, breakfast really is the most important meal of the day, so it doesn't matter what time of day you order it. Want scrambled eggs at 2.30pm? Most cafés will be happy to oblige[15]. Even the ones that switch over to a lunch menu at midday still sneak a few breakfast-style items in for good measure[16].

6. ___________________________________

Sydney has an international reputation as a go-to destination for sun-seekers, and we certainly do catch quite a few rays here in the Land Down Under. But be warned, Sydney can dish out its fair share[17] of wild weather too. Courtesy of a sub-tropical climate, torrential rain and

---

[6] a seasoned walker in search of a more challenging trek: ein erfahrener Wanderer auf der Suche nach einer anspruchsvollen Wanderung

[7] fringes: Fransen; hier: Außenbezirke

[8] stellar ferry trip: Sternfahrt mit der Fähre

[9] chuggers: Kähne, Dampfer

[10] chequered past: wechselvolle Geschichte

[11] inexplicably scrapped tram network: unerklärlich verschrottetes Straßenbahnnetz

[12] to be prone to: anfällig sein für

[13] are aiming to streamline the customer experience: zielen darauf ab, das Kundenerlebnis zu optimieren

[14] to keep services slick: um die Dienste reibungslos zu halten

[15] to oblige: sich verpflichten

[16] sneak a few breakfast-style items in for good measure: ein paar frühstücksähnliche Dinge als Zugabe einbauen

[17] to dish out its fair share: seinen Teil beitragen

summer storms are not uncommon here, and can roll in from the Tasman Sea, dropping a deluge on the city[18], without much notice. So, even if the sun is shining and the skies are clear in the morning, you'd be wise to check the forecast before heading out for the day. And if rain is on the horizon, we suggest a rain-poncho over an umbrella: even the sturdiest brollies[19] don't last long during Sydney's epic downpours[20].

7. ______________________________

Many parts of the country are currently experiencing unprecedented droughts[21], especially in New South Wales. This has led to some of the worst bushfire conditions ever recorded in Australia, with huge, uncontrolled blazes on Sydney's outskirts releasing smoke and haze that can linger over the city[22] for days or even weeks. If you're going out of town, particularly if you're heading into the bush, make sure you check the day's fire hazard warnings, and when the smoke gets thick in the city – and at times it can be choking[23] – keep an eye on the air quality rating in your area.

[This text has been taken from the TimeOut Magazine Online; it has been shortened for the purpose of this exercise; 19 December 2019: https://www.timeout.com/sydney/travel/travel-tips-every-first-time-sydney-visitor-needs-to-know]

a) Assign each paragraph a heading from below. NOTE: There are two extra headings which you do not need

A: Ferries really are a thing here

B: Sydney is Australia's greatest city

C: Summer is bushfire season

D: Don't worry about the weather

E: But you can also get breakfast all day

F: Everyone needs an Opal

G: Leave plenty of time to get places

H: The sun doesn't always shine here

I: But much of the city is easily walkable

____/7

b) Answer the following questions in short sentences

1. What is an Opal Card?

____

[18] a deluge: eine Überschwemmung
[19] the sturdiest brollies: die robustesten Regenschirme
[20] epic downpours: Wolkenbrüche
[21] unprecedented droughts: nie dagewesene Dürreperioden
[22] haze that can linger over the city: Dunst, der über der Stadt verweilen kann
[23] it can be choking: es kann erstickend sein

2. What is the problem with public transport in Sydney?

___

3. Why is Sydney the ideal place for breakfast-lovers?

___

4. What should you do before you head out and explore the city (even when it is sunny)?

___

___/8

c) Decide whether the following statement is true (T), false (F) or not in the text (NT)

1. You need an Opal Card when using trains in Sydney.

O T O F O NT

2. Sydney is very large compared to other international cities.

O T O F O NT

3. Every resident in Sydney loves breakfast.

O T O F O NT

4. Sydney is a popular destination for tourists who love the sun.

O T O F O NT

5. Bushfires cannot always be controlled.

O T O F O NT ___/5

II. Vocabulary

Explain the following words from unit 1 in your own words

1. resident: ___
2. victim: ___
3. refugee: ___
4. desperate: ___
5. wealthy: ___

___/10

III. Translation

Translate these sentences into English

1. Letzten Monat haben wir das Auto reparieren lassen.

___

2. Meine Eltern ließen mich nach der Schule mein Zimmer aufräumen.

___

3. Ich hoffe, dass ich bis zum Ende meiner Schulzeit genug Geld habe, um nach Italien zu reisen.

____

____

4. Das Pro-Kopf-Einkommen in Australien ist eines der höchsten der Welt.

____

5. Ich denke, ich werde im Ausland studieren.

____

____/10

IV. English Language Proficiency / Grammar

Spot 20 mistakes in the text below. Underline and correct them

Tanya hopes that at the time she finishes her last exams, she will earn enough money in her part-time job to travel to sydney. She is sure that she would be having a good time there. She will be spend two weeks in the City. Tanya hopes that she will improve her English skills at the time she arrived in Sydney. If not, she will be struggling with understanding the peoples there. Tanya will be staying in a very cheep hostel in Sydney and she would not be having a room for herself. Fortunatelly, her best friend will have been travelling with her, so she won't be all alone. However, her Friend will not save enough money on the time they arrive in australia, either. Perhaps they should have choosen a different city, because Sydney is expensive

____/20

Total points ____/60

Good luck !

Lösung: 1. Schulaufgabe aus dem Englischen

I. Reading Comprehension

Read the text "Travel tips every first time Sydney visitor needs to know" carefully and answer the questions below. It is advised to read through the questions first. Pay attention to the footnotes as there might be some words you do not know

Travel tips every first time Sydney visitor needs to know – Things to know the day you land

1. Everyone needs an Opal → F

2. But much of the city is easily walkable → I

3. Ferries really are a thing here → A

4. Leave plenty of time to get places → G

5. But you can also get breakfast all day → E

6. The sun doesn't always shine here → H

7. Summer is bushfire season → C

a) Assign each paragraph a heading from below. NOTE: There are two extra headings which you do not need

A: Ferries really are a thing here

B: Sydney is Australia's greatest city

C: Summer is bushfire season

D: Don't worry about the weather

E: But you can also get breakfast all day

F: Everyone needs an Opal

G: Leave plenty of time to get places

H: The sun doesn't always shine here

I: But much of the city is easily walkable

b) Answer the following questions in short sentences

1. What is an Opal Card?

An Opal Card is a payment method for public transportation (in Sydney).

2. What is the problem with public transport in Sydney?

Public transport in Sydney is often delayed.

Tipps & Tricks: Beispiele (z.B. *trains*) müssen hier nicht genannt werden.

3. Why is Sydney the ideal place for breakfast-lovers?

Many/Most cafés offer breakfast after noon.

4. What should you do before you head out and explore the city (even when it is sunny)?

You should always check the weather forecast.

Tipps & Tricks: *all day* zu nennen anstelle von *after noon* wäre auch in Ordnung. Den Regenschirm mitzunehmen wäre auch eine akzeptable Antwort.

c) Decide whether the following statement is true (T), false (F) or not in the text (NT)

1. You need an Opal Card when using trains in Sydney.

○ T ✔ F ○ NT

Tipps & Tricks: Nur in Bussen ist eine *Opal Card* unabdingbar, aber nicht generell.

2. Sydney is very large compared to other international cities.

○ T ✔ F ○ NT

Tipps & Tricks: *compact* = kompakt; die Stadt kann trotz ihrer hohen Bevölkerung leicht zu Fuß erkundet werden.

3. Every resident in Sydney loves breakfast.

○ T ○ F ✔ NT

Tipps & Tricks: Das mag vielleicht so sein, steht aber so nicht im Text.

4. Sydney is a popular destination for tourists who love the sun.

✔ T ○ F ○ NT

5. Bushfires cannot always be controlled.

✔ T ○ F ○ NT

II. Vocabulary

Explain the following words from unit 1 in your own words

1. resident: *a person who lives in a particular place and/or who has his home there*

Tipps & Tricks: *residence* bezeichnet wiederum den Wohnsitz.

2. victim: *a person who has been attacked, injured or killed as the result of a crime, disease or else*

3. refugee: *a person who has been forced to leave their country or home, because of war, political prosecution or else*

Tipps & Tricks: *to take refuge* → Zuflucht suchen/nehmen

4. desperate: *feeling or showing that you have little hope (and are ready to do anything without worrying about danger to yourself or others)*

Tipps & Tricks: *desperation* = Verzweiflung

5. wealthy: *having a lot of money, possessions, etc.*

Tipps & Tricks: Synonym: *rich*

III. Translation

Translate these sentences into English

1. Letzten Monat haben wir das Auto reparieren lassen.

1. Last month we had the car repaired.

Tipps & Tricks: etwas machen lassen → *have something done*

2. Meine Eltern ließen mich nach der Schule mein Zimmer aufräumen.

2. My parents made me clean up my room after school.

Tipps & Tricks: jemanden dazu bringen, etwas zu tun → *make sombody do something*

3. Ich hoffe, dass ich bis zum Ende meiner Schulzeit genug Geld habe, um nach Italien zu reisen.

3. I hope that by the time I finish school, I will be having enough money to travel to Italy.

Tipps & Tricks: siehe ***Future progressive*** (s.S. 25)

4. Das Pro-Kopf-Einkommen in Australien ist eines der höchsten der Welt.

4. The per capita income in Australia is one of the highest in the world.

5. Ich denke, ich werde im Ausland studieren.

5. I think I will study overseas.

Tipps & Tricks: oder man sagt: *study abroad*

IV. English Language Proficiency / Grammar

Spot 20 mistakes in the text below. Underline and correct them

Tanya hopes that at (1) the time she finishes her last exams, she will earn (2) enough money in her part-time job to travel to sydney (3). She is sure that she would (4) be having a good time there. She will be spend (5) two weeks in the City (6). Tanya hopes that she will improve (7) her English skills at (8) the time she arrived (9) in Sydney. If not, she will be struggling with understanding the peoples (10) there. Tanya will be staying in a very cheep (11) hostel in Sydney and she would (12) not be having a room for herself. Fortunatelly (13), her best friend will have been (14) travelling with her, so she won't be all alone. However, her Friend (15) will not save (16) enough money on (17) the time they arrive in australia (18), either. Perhaps they should have choosen (19) a different city, because Sydney is expensive_(20)

by (1);
will have earned (2);
Sydney (3); will (4);
spending (5); city (6);
have improved (7); by (8);
arrives (9);
people (10);
cheap (11);
will (12); Fortunately (13);
be (14);
friend (15);
have saved (16); by (17);
Australia (18); chosen (19);
. (20)

Tipps & Tricks (zu):
(1), (8), (17): *by the time* beschreibt hier **zu der Zeit, bis zu diesem Zeitpunkt**.
By the time... ist eine Wendung, der ein Satz folgt, der sich auf einen Zeitrahmen bezieht, um den Fortschritt oder den Abschluss der Aktivität im Hauptsatz anzuzeigen; oder der eine Aktivität mit einer Dauer und einem Endpunkt umfasst.
By the time ist oft ein Signalwort bzw. eine Signalwendung für das ***Future perfect***.
Bei anderen Präpositionen für eine Zeitangabe gilt für gewöhnlich:
at → präzise Zeit (z.B. *We meet at 10am*)
in → für Monate, Jahre, Jahrhunderte und lange Zeiträume (z.B. *Let's meet in August*)
on → für bestimmte Tage und Daten (z.B. *Do you work on Saturdays?*)
(2), (7), (16): ***Future perfect:*** Beschreibt eine Aktion / Handlung die schon vor einem bestimmten Zeitpunkt in der Zukunft passiert sein wird. → *will/will not + have + Verb_ past participle*
(4), (5), (12), (14): ***Future progressive:*** Beschreibt eine Aktion/Handlung in der Zukunft die definitiv (bzw. äußerst wahrscheinlich) passieren wird. → *will/will not + be + Verb_ing*

1. Schulaufgabe aus dem Englischen

Name: ____________________

Stoff: Unit 1-2

I. Reading Comprehension

Read the following text carefully and answer the questions below

Study: the Fridays for Future movement is facing its limits

Fridays for Future is playing a pivotal role[24] in mobilizing global climate action, yet the movement is now facing limits imposed by its own rhetoric[25], according to a new study in Nature Climate Change.

The key point of the critique by Darrick Evensen, an environmental social-psychologist at the University of Edinburgh, is simple yet important: the movement's young Swedish founder Greta Thunberg's insistence on science as the only guidance for action[26] can be its own trap. Scientific evidence warns us and helps us make better choices; however, science alone is insufficient to help us make ethical decisions outside hard data and facts, Evensen suggests.

First of all, approaching science as a final arbiter[27] "misunderstands the role of knowledge in ethical action" leading us towards "unquestioned scientific progressivism of the modern era". It takes for granted science as such, forgetting about the variety of values and aspirations of scientists and decisionmakers alike. While scientific fact is presented as non-negotiable truth, almost all the choices we make in regards to climate action are often based on economic considerations such as the price of renewables.

Second, path dependencies, institutions lagging behind[28], and the fossil fuel lobby are among factors that slow down effective action even as we try to make scientific facts fit a particular agenda and certain interests. As Evensen notes, the "scientization" of particular choices based on individual values is an error even the most respectful academics commit on regular basis. Scientists are also prone to underestimating the worst possible impacts for fear of not being objective.

Finally, rational thinking and economic reasoning, which are so favored by scientists, don't nearly work as well as inspiring people and telling them imaginative stories of a different future. To make the new world possible, we can't wait for economics to tell us that investing in climate action will be a good bargain. We need creativity to imagine how a different future could look like, as well as bold leadership to make it happen.

This research is in line with other recent studies that underline the point that on science alone, without accounting for a religious and cultural diversity of societies, can harm public support for climate action. Many potential supporters could even turn into denialists. On the other hand, a strict focus on forecasting and business-as-usual scenarios limit innovative thinking, while community planning based on back-casting from desired futures often gives birth to the most captivating visions of a more liveable and thriving planet[29].

---

[24] pivotal role: zentrale Rolle, Schlüsselrolle

[25] the movement is now facing limits imposed by its own rhetoric: die Bewegung stößt nun an Grenzen, die ihr von ihrer eigenen Rhetorik auferlegt werden

[26] insistence on science as the only guidance for action: Beharren auf der Wissenschaft als einzige Handlungsanleitung

[27] final arbiter: letzte Instanz, endgültiger Vermittler

[28] institutions lagging behind: rückständige Institutionen

[29] thriving planet: blühender Planet

Science can tell us what can happen if we don't act and how fast we need to change. It can also tell us about the benefits of richer biodiversity and a more stable climate. It can help us count how many lives will be saved and which cultural heritage might be lost. Science can even calculate the probability of different proposals being embraced by society and the potential effectiveness of sustainable[30] marketing campaigns.

However, when science meets people it needs vision and passion. It requires a feeling of personal responsibility and strong ethical commitment. It needs to acknowledge cultural diversity, political context, and varieties of local worldviews. For decades, evidence-based science on climate change has been available, but only active public participation and strong pressure from civil society have made the Paris agreement a reality.
As Evensen notes, quoting Nobel Laureate Lord Bertrand Russell: "Almost all the questions of interest to speculative minds are such as science cannot answer." And he is sure that climate change is a question of this kind. If we want science to really help us, we need to go beyond science alone. It might be the time Fridays for Future started using this insight effectively.
Thunberg herself admits that she says what people are ready to hear and understand, brimming[31] with ideas for how to reshape the current global system, from the broader implementation of the circular economy to wide-scale urban rewilding. Fridays for Future activists are well aware of the global sustainability discourse that goes far beyond the "divest from coal" and "100% renewables" rhetoric.
It might now be time they stepped beyond what people are used to hearing and into a world of how much more is possible.

[This text has been taken from Sustainability Times; 31 May 2019: https://www.sustainability-times.com/environmental-protection/study-the-fridays-for-future-movement-is-facing-its-limits/]

---

[30] sustainable, sustainability: nachhaltig, Nachhaltigkeit
[31] brimming: randvoll mit

a) Decide which of the following statements is true (T), false (F) or not in the text (NT)

1. FFF (Fridays for Future) has played a very important role in mobilising climate action.
O T
O F
O NT

2. Darrick Evensen works in Scotland.
O T
O F
O NT

3. According to Evensen, only science will help us making better ethical decisions.
O T
O F
O NT

4. According to Evensen, science should not be viewed as the final arbiter.
O T
O F
O NT

5. Scientific facts are sometimes driven by certain interests.
O T
O F
O NT

6. Rational thinking and economic reasoning do not always get through to people.
O T
O F
O NT

7. Focusing on science only, can sometimes negatively affect public support for climate action.
O T
O F
O NT

8. Science cannot tell us what happens if we don't act.
O T
O F
O NT

9. People generally believe in science.
O T
O F
O NT

10. FFF will further rely on science only in the future.
- ◯ T
- ◯ F
- ◯ NT

____/10

b) Answer the following questions. Try to use your own words

1. What does Darrick Evensen criticize about FFF and Greta Thunberg?

____

____

____

____

____

2. Why does Evensen think that science cannot solve all problems?

____

____

____

____

____/10

II. English Language Proficiency / Grammar

Spot 2 mistakes in each sentence and correct them

1. The magazines which were send to us are for my mother

____

2. Tanya stood at the busstation talk to her best friend.

____

3. David told me that his brother had flewn to New York last year.

____

4. Tanya told me that she hadn't have time to make her homework.

____

5. Will he has given up his dream of travel to London? No, he won't.

____

6. I studied for the english exam for more than six hours.

____

7. Causing a lot of pollution the aviation industry has came into the focus of activists.

8. I cought him shout.

9. Tanyas parents told him that there are worried about him.

10. My mother wanted to know if I am nervous with the exam.

____/20

III. Translation

Translate the following sentences into English. Pay particular attention to vocabulary from unit 1 & 2. You can get 3 points for each sentence

1. Meinem Kumpel ist Nachhaltigkeit egal.

2. Fortschritt wird immer mit Umweltschutz assoziiert.

3. Große Teile Australiens sind unbewohnbar geworden.

4. Das Pro-Kopf-Einkommen in Deutschland ist viel höher als in Osteuropa.

5. Viele Menschen machen sich Sorgen um den starken Anstieg von Treibhausgasen.

____/15

Total points ____/55

Good luck !

Lösung: 1. Schulaufgabe aus dem Englischen

I. Reading Comprehension

Read the text "Study: the Fridays for Future movement is facing its limits" carefully and answer the questions below
a) Decide which of the following statements is true (T), false (F) or not in the text (NT)

1. FFF (Fridays for Future) has played a very important role in mobilising climate action.
✔ T
○ F
○ NT

2. Darrick Evensen works in Scotland.
✔ T
○ F
○ NT
Tipps & Tricks: Da er an der Universität in Edinburgh arbeitet, ist diese Aussage richtig.

3. According to Evensen, only science will help us making better ethical decisions.
○ T
✔ F
○ NT

4. According to Evensen, science should not be viewed as the final arbiter.
✔ T
○ F
○ NT

5. Scientific facts are sometimes driven by certain interests.
✔ T
○ F
○ NT

6. Rational thinking and economic reasoning do not always get through to people.
✔ T
○ F
○ NT
Tipps & Tricks: sondern eher Geschichten über eine imaginierte Zukunft.

7. Focusing on science only, can sometimes negatively affect public support for climate action.
✔ T
○ F
○ NT

8. Science cannot tell us what happens if we don't act.
○ T
✔ F
○ NT

9. People generally believe in science.
○ T
○ F
✔ NT

Tipps & Tricks: Darüber gibt es keine Aussage im Text.

10. FFF will further rely on science only in the future.
○ T
○ F
✔ NT

Tipps & Tricks: Dies mag so sein, wird aber nicht im Text erwähnt.

b) Answer the following questions. Be brief

1. What does Darrick Evensen criticize about FFF and Greta Thunberg?

Evensen criticizes that FFF and Thunberg focus on science too much. He believes that science alone cannot help us make better ethical decisions.

2. Why does Evensen think that science cannot solve all problems?

He thinks that science needs to also recognize cultural diversity, political context, and different worldviews. When science meets people, it needs to be responsible and contain a strong ethical commitment.

Tipps & Tricks: 2,5 Punkte für den Inhalt; 2,5 Punkte für Grammatik / Syntax

II. English Language Proficiency / Grammar

Spot 2 mistakes in each sentence and correct them

1. The magazines which were send to us are for my mother
1. The magazines which were *sent* to us are for my mother *[.]*

2. Tanya stood at the busstation talk to her best friend.
2. Tanya stood at the *bus station talking* to her best friend.

3. David told me that his brother had flewn to New York last year.
3. David told me that his brother had *flown* to New York *the year before.*

Tipps & Tricks: Zeit- / Ortsangaben verändern sich in der indirekten Rede.
Hier: *last year* → *the year before.*

4. Tanya told me that she hadn't have time to make her homework.
4. Tanya told me that she hadn't *had* time to *do* her homework.

5. Will he has given up his dream of travel to London? No, he won't.
5. Will he *have* given up his dream of *travelling* to London? No, he won't.

6. I studied for the english exam for more than six hours.
6. I *have been studying* for the *English* exam for more than six hours.

Tipps & Tricks: *for*" ist hier ein Signalwort und weist auf ***Present perfect progressive*** hin.

7. Causing a lot of pollution the aviation industry has came into the focus of activists.
7. Causing a lot of pollution *[,]* the aviation industry has *come* into the focus of activists.

8. I caught him shout.
8. I *cought* him *shouting*.

9. Tanyas parents told him that they are worried about him.
9. Tanya*[']*s parents told him that they *were* worried about him.

Tipps & Tricks: In indirekter Rede: *are* → *were*

10. My mother wanted to know if I am nervous with the exam.
10. My mother wanted to know if I *was* nervous *about* the exam.

Tipps & Tricks: In indirekter Rede: *am* → *was*
(siehe S. 53)

III. Translation

Translate the following sentences into English. Pay particular attention to vocabulary from unit 1 & 2. You can get 3 points for each sentence

1. Meinem Kumpel ist Nachhaltigkeit egal.
My mate doesn't care about sustainability.
2. Fortschritt wird immer mit Umweltschutz assoziiert.
Progress is always associated with environmental protection.
3. Große Teile Australiens sind unbewohnbar geworden.
Large parts of Australia have become uninhabitable.
4. Das Pro-Kopf-Einkommen in Deutschland ist viel höher als in Osteuropa.
The per capita income in Germany is much higher than in Eastern Europe.
Tipps & Tricks: Alternativ: *Germany's per capita income is.....*
5. Viele Menschen machen sich Sorgen um den starken Anstieg von Treibhausgasen.
Many people are concerned about the sharp/big increase of greenhouse gases.
Tipps & Tricks: Alternativ: *are worried about .....*

2. Schulaufgabe aus dem Englischen

Name: ____________________________

Stoff: Unit 2

I. Reading Comprehension / Listening Comprehension

Read the following text carefully and answer the questions below

How sustainable are ‚eco' brand high street fashions?

There's a new trend among popular fashion brands: „eco friendly" collections. Organic cotton is everywhere this summer, but is the label just a marketing strategy?

This summer's high street fashions have more in common than styles and colors. From the pink puff-sleeved dream[32] going for just €19.99 ($22.52) at H&M, to Zara's elegant €12.95 halter-neck dress[33], clothing stores are alive with cheap organic cotton.
„Sustainable" collections with aspirational own-brand names[34] like C&A's „Wear the change," Zara's „join life" or H&M's „CONSCIOUS" are offering cheap fashion and a clean environmental conscience. Such, at least, is the message. But is it really that simple?

Going green, or just greenwashing?

„Fashion brands are capitalizing on the fact that consumers are interested in buying fairly and ecologically produced items," said Katrin Wenz, an expert in agriculture at Friends of the Earth Germany (BUND). „Organic cotton is certainly a step in the right direction, because neither genetic modification nor synthetic pesticides can be used in its production. But these own-brand sustainability labels rarely tell us anything about what happens later on in the production chain."
Viola Wohlgemuth, a textiles expert at Greenpeace says companies create their sustainability labels and criteria themselves. „Sustainability is not a protected or specific term, which leaves the door wide open for so-called greenwashing," she told DW (Deutsche Welle – News and current affairs from Germany).

Independent certifications trustworthier[35]

Both experts emphasize[36] that independent environmental certifications offer a better indicator of a product's eco credentials[37], including labor conditions for workers involved in production. Examples include the Global Organic Textile Standard label (GOTS) and the IVN Best certification, which is awarded by the International Association of Natural Textile Industry (IVN).
Heike Hess, head of IVN's Berlin branch, says using organic cotton alone „is not enough to make fashion really sustainable," and that producing clothes involves a more involved production chain. After being grown in the fields, cotton fibers[38] have to be separated from their seeds, dyed[39], printed and sewn[40] to create finished items of clothing.

---

[32] pink puff-sleeved dream: Traum mit rosa Puffärmeln
[33] halter-neck dress: Kleid mit Nackenband
[34] aspirational own-brand names: aufstrebende Eigenmarkennamen
[35] trustworthier: vertrauenswürdiger, zuverlässiger
[36] emphasize: hervorheben
[37] credentials: Berechtigungsnachweise
[38] cotton fibers: Baumwollfasern
[39] dyed: eingefärbt
[40] sewn: genäht

„Ecological and social standards are important at every stage of production,“ Hess said. „That includes minimizing the use of harmful[41] chemicals, managing water usage and waste, limiting CO_2 emissions and ensuring human rights, fair wages, protections for workers and much more. Only then can fashion really be called sustainable.“
And that comes at a price. Organic cotton summer dresses certified with the GOTS label usually cost somewhere between €60-100.

Water polluted and wasted
Textile production often uses harmful chemicals, especially during the wet processing stage when threads[42] are formed, dyed and woven[43], says Wohlgemuth. According to the UN Environment Programme, around 20 % of global wastewater is generated during textile dyeing[44] and processing. Communities and ecosystems in textile producing countries across Asia are worst affected[45].
Since launching its ‚Detox My Fashion‘ campaign in 2011, Greenpeace has secured commitments[46] from some 80 global companies in the fashion industry to eliminate hazardous chemicals by the end of this year.
But that alone doesn’t imply sustainability. Growing cotton also requires a huge amount of water and vast areas of land, says Sabine Ferenschild from the Südwind Institute for Economics and Ecumenism[47] in Bonn.
„Organic cotton is only sustainable when grown in rainy regions such as India, and planted in combination with food crops rather than in competition with them,“ she said. „But we have seen that cotton farming is increasingly being shifted to desert regions. That can never be sustainable.“

Eco collections remain a market niche
Ferenschild is critical of major fashion brands’ attempts to go green with their own criteria and labeling for certain products, while the majority of what they’re selling is still produced conventionally.
Germany is pursuing[48] a new approach to green certification with its government-backed[49] ‚Green Button‘ label. A company can only use the label if all its products comply with high environmental and labor standards. These standards are not as strict as those demanded by organic certifiers, but experts say the ‚Green Button‘ label is a step in the right direction, as it prevents producers offloading responsibility to subcontractors[50] in the production chain.

An ‚eco‘ dress for €20: Too good to be true?
According to the Bremen Cotton Exchange, organic cotton costs between 10 and 50 % more than conventional cotton. Premium fibers boost[51] prices the most; the raw material is not necessarily the most important factor in terms of cost.

---

41 harmful: schädlich
42 threads: Fäden
43 woven: gewebt, gewoben
44 dyeing: färben, Einfärben
45 worst affected: am stärksten betroffen
46 commitments: Verpflichtungen
47 Ecumenism: Ökologie
48 is pursuing: verfolgt
49 government-backed: staatlich gestützt
50 subcontractors: Subunternehmer
51 to boost: erhöhen

Global fashion brands like H&M are able to keep their prices down, even for the products in their ‚sustainable' ranges, due to the huge volume of items they produce, textiles expert Ferenschild told DW.
H&M uses its own ‚CONSCIOUS' label for products which contain „at least 50 percent sustainable materials, such as organic cotton and recycled polyester." It is not clear to consumers what percentage of organic cotton is used in the items labeled as such. In response to DW's request for clarification, H&M wrote: „Across our entire range, H&M uses 16 percent organic cotton according to our most recent figures[52]."
According to the Bremen Cotton Exchange, just 0.7 percent of the global cotton harvest in the 2017/18 season was organic.

The real problem is one of quantity
Even if the big fashion brands wanted to move further towards truly sustainable production, current consumption habits would make that almost impossible. The real problem is that far too many clothes are being produced. According to a 2015 Greenpeace study, there are more than five billion items of clothing in German wardrobes alone.
„A party top is worn on average just 1.7 times," said Viola Wohlgemuth. „Fast fashion is the SUV of the fashion industry. It will never be sustainable. The fashion industry needs to shift away[53] from production and towards service provision."
There are already some examples of this: outdoor brands offering to repair products, jeans companies selling second-hand items alongside new, sustainably produced pairs. Even fast-fashion giant H&M's website now has tips on how to care for and repair for clothes.
But to be successful, this shift would need consumers to get on board. And that, says Katrin Wenz from Friends of the Earth Germany would mean „buying fewer and longer-lasting items, repairing damaged clothing, passing on clothes you no longer wear and choosing to buy second hand."
Perhaps then, sustainability in fashion could be more than just another trend.

[This text has been taken from Deutsche Welle; 06 July 2020: https://www.dw.com/en/environment-fashion-hm-zara-clothes-sustainable-organic-cotton/a-53916904]

[52] most recent figures: aktuellste Zahlen
[53] to shift away: wegschieben

a) Answer the questions below. Note: Each of the questions is worth 5 points, so your answer will have to be a bit more comprehensive

1. Why is it doubtful that new collections from H&M, Zara, and others are really eco-friendly?

____

____

____

____

2. According to the article, how can fashion be more sustainable (and eco-friendly)?

____

____

____

____

____/10

b) Multiple Answer: Tick the correct answers for each question; Note: 'Multiple Answer' means that none, one, two, or all three answers could be correct

1. What do current summer collections of H&M, Zara, and others have in common?
- ○ They claim to be sustainable.
- ○ They are very colourful.
- ○ They are inexpensive.

2. What do many customers increasingly pay attention to when buying fashion?
- ○ Synthetic
- ○ Fair Trade
- ○ Ecology

3. Many 'Fast Fashion Brands' do what?
- ○ Work with organisations who award independent environmental certifications
- ○ Pay very close attention to labour conditions in the countries where they produce
- ○ Only use organic cotton in the production

4. Which of these certifications are renowned for being independent and sustainable?
- ○ IVN
- ○ GOTS
- ○ BUND

5. What has to be considered when producing fashion according to ecological and social standards?
- ○ Chemicals should not be used.
- ○ Water use should be decreased.
- ○ Fair wages for workers

6. What is the aim of the ‚Detox My Fashion‘ campaign?
○ Making fashion more expensive
○ Using more organic cotton
○ Obtaining commitments from many fashion companies

7. What is the problem with growing sustainable organic cotton?
○ It needs a lot of rain.
○ It cannot be grown everywhere.
○ It needs a lot of land.

8. Why is Ferenschild very critical of major fashion brand's attempt to go green?
○ Their fashion is too cheap.
○ Most items are still produced conventionally.
○ They create their own green labels.

9. Which statement(s) about organic cotton is/are true?
○ It is very cheap.
○ It is sustainable not matter where it is grown.
○ It accounts for less than one percent of the global cotton harvest.

10. Which statement(s) about fast fashion is/are true?
○ It can be sustainable.
○ Fast fashion pieces are not worn very often.
○ Too many clothes are produced.

____/10

c) Decide which of the following statements is true or false

1. Going green is the same as greenwashing.
○ True
○ False

2. Synthetic pesticides are not allowed in the production of organic cotton.
○ True
○ False

3. Sustainability is a protected term.
○ True
○ False

4. Hess believes that organic cotton is the solution to all problems.
○ True
○ False

5. Future fashion production needs to decrease CO_2 emissions.
○ True
○ False

6. The textile industry is responsible for at least 1/5 of the global wastewater.
- ○ True
- ○ False

7. Most fashion is currently being produced in Asia.
- ○ True
- ○ False

8. Cotton which is produced in the desert is unsustainable.
- ○ True
- ○ False

9. Germany's ‚Green Button' label is the strictest there is.
- ○ True
- ○ False

10. People's buying habits are part of the problem.
- ○ True
- ○ False

____/10

II. Vocabulary and English Language Proficiency / Grammar

a) Rewrite the following sentences by using a participle construction

1. The magazines which were sent to us are for my mother.

____

2. Tanya stood at the bus station and talked to her best friend.

____

3. The exam was written at this school. The exam was very important.

____

4. She was very smart. She became a scientist.

____

5. The man who carried a gun crossed the street.

____

____/10

b) Find synonyms or antonyms for the following words

1. often (synonym): ____________________
2. in the end, at last (synonym): ______________________
3. good (antonym): ______________________
4. respect (antonym): ______________________
5. to dye (antonym): ______________________ ____/5

III. Text Production

The article presented in this exam's reading comprehension provided you with a lot of information on the problem concerning fast fashion and sustainability. Now imagine the following: To make fashion more sustainable, the parliament of Ruritania has just decided that from now on every piece of clothes will cost twice the amount it costs now. A pair of sweat pants, for example, now cost 40€ instead of 20€. Do you think that is a good idea? Make a clear argument on either yes or no. Write NO LESS than 60 words

____/10

Total points ____/55

Good luck !

Lösung: 2. Schulaufgabe aus dem Englischen

I. Reading Comprehension

Read the text "How sustainable are ‚eco' brand high street fashions?" carefully

a) Answer the questions below. Note: Each of the questions is worth 5 points, so your answer will have to be a bit more comprehensive

1. Why is it doubtful that new collections from H&M, Zara, and others are really eco-friendly?

The companies in question only claim to be eco-friendly. Most clothing items from fast fashion brands are still produced conventionally. In addition to that, green labels from those companies are not independent, meaning that it is not clear whether those green labels are truly green and sustainable.

> **Tipps & Tricks**
> Was in jedem Fall erwähnt werden sollte: 1. Produktion immer noch weitgehend konventionell. 2. Grüne Etiketten sind nicht von unabhängigen Instituten vergeben. Sonstige Punkte: Kleidung ist zu billig um nachhaltig zu sein.

2. According to the article, how can fashion be more sustainable (and eco-friendly)?

Customers will have to spend more money on fashion and buy less instead of more. Fashion brands need not only focus on production and selling but also on service provision. Moreover, clothing items which are broken should not be thrown away, but repaired instead. Buying clothes second hand could also prove to have a positive impact on sustainability.

> **Tipps & Tricks**
> Was in jedem Fall erwähnt werden sollte: 1. Weniger Kleidung kaufen 2. Kleidung sollte länger getragen werden. Sonstige Punkte: Kleidung gebraucht kaufen; kaputte Kleidung reparieren

b) Multiple Answer: Tick the correct answers for each question. Note: 'Multiple Answer' means that none, one, two, or all three answers could be correct

1. What do current summer collections of H&M, Zara, and others have in common?

✔ They claim to be sustainable.
○ They are very colourful.
✔ They are inexpensive.

2. What do many customers increasingly pay attention to when buying fashion?

○ Synthetic
✔ Fair Trade
✔ Ecology

3. Many 'Fast Fashion Brands' do what?
- ○ Work with organisations who award independent environmental certifications
- ○ Pay very close attention to labour conditions in the countries where they produce
- ○ Only use organic cotton in the production

Tipps & Tricks: Keine der Antworten trifft auf Fast Fashion Brands zu.

4. Which of these certifications are renowned for being independent and sustainable?
- ✔ IVN
- ✔ GOTS
- ○ BUND

Tipps & Tricks: BUND vergibt keine Nachhaltigkeitszertifikate.

5. What has to be considered when producing fashion according to ecological and social standards?
- ○ Chemicals should not be used.
- ✔ Water use should be decreased.
- ✔ Fair wages for workers

Tipps & Tricks: Im Text ist die Rede von *harmful chemicals*, nicht Chemikalien generell.

6. What is the aim of the ‚Detox My Fashion' campaign?
- ○ Making fashion more expensive.
- ○ Using more organic cotton.
- ✔ Obtaining commitments from many fashion companies.

Tipps & Tricks: Laut Text, bis jetzt von 80 Firmen

7. What is the problem with growing sustainable organic cotton?
- ✔ It needs a lot of rain.
- ✔ It cannot be grown everywhere.
- ✔ It needs a lot of land.

8. Why is Ferenschild very critical of major fashion brand's attempt to go green?
- ○ Their fashion is too cheap.
- ✔ Most items are still produced conventionally.
- ✔ They create their own green labels.

9. Which statement(s) about organic cotton is/are true?
- ○ It is very cheap.
- ○ It is sustainable not matter where it is grown.
- ✔ It accounts for less than one percent of the global cotton harvest.

Tipps & Tricks: 0,7% um genau zu sein.

10. Which statement(s) about fast fashion is/are true?
○ It can be sustainable.
✔ Fast fashion pieces are not worn very often.
✔ Too many clothes are produced.

c) Decide which of the following statements is true or false

1. Going green is the same as greenwashing.
○ True
✔ False

2. Synthetic pesticides are not allowed in the production of organic cotton.
✔ True
○ False

3. Sustainability is a protected term.
○ True
✔ False

4. Hess believes that organic cotton is the solution to all problems.
○ True
✔ False

Tipps & Tricks: Es ist ein Teil der Lösung, aber es muss noch sehr viel mehr passieren.

5. Future fashion production needs to decrease CO_2 emissions.
✔ True
○ False

6. The textile industry is responsible for at least 1/5 of the global wastewater.
✔ True
○ False

Tipps & Tricks: Im Text ist die Rede von 20% was wiederum 1/5 entspricht.

7. Most fashion is currently being produced in Asia.
✔ True
○ False

8. Cotton which is produced in the desert is unsustainable.
✔ True
○ False

9. Germany's ‚Green Button' label is the strictest there is.
○ True
✔ False

Tipps & Tricks: Das deutsche 'Green Button' Zertifikat ist nicht so streng wie das mancher anderer.

10. People's buying habits are part of the problem.

✔ True
◯ False

Tipps & Tricks: Wahr, da die Leute gewohnt sind viel (und) günstig zu kaufen.

II. Vocabulary and English Language Proficiency / Grammar

a) Rewrite the following sentences by using participle constructions

1. The magazines which were sent to us are for my mother.

The magazines sent to us are for my mother.

2. Tanya stood at the bus station and talked to her best friend.

Tanya stood at the bus station talking to her best friend.

3. The exam was written at this school. The exam was very important.

The exam written at this school was very important.

4. She was very smart. She became a scientist.

Being very smart, she became a scientist.

5. The man who carried a gun crossed the street.

The man carrying a gun crossed the street.

Tipps & Tricks
Partizipialkonstruktionen werden vielfach zur **Verkürzung von Sätzen** verwendet.
Bedingung für die Verkürzung von Relativsätzen ist, dass das Subjekt im ursprünglichen Haupt- und Nebensatz identisch ist.
Beispiel: Anstelle von: *The man who is shaking his head is my father*
die verkürzte Form: *The man shaking his head is my father.*

b) Find synonyms or antonyms for the following words

1. often (synonym): *frequent*
2. in the end, at last (synonym): *eventually*
3. good (antonym): *evil*
4. respect (antonym): *disrespect*
5. to dye (antonym): *to bleach*

III. Text Production

The article presented in this exam's reading comprehension provided you with a lot of information on the problem concerning fast fashion and sustainability. Now imagine the following: To make fashion more sustainable, the parliament of Ruritania has just decided that from now on every piece of clothes will cost twice the amount it costs now. A pair of sweat pants, for example, now cost 40€ instead of 20€. Do you think that is a good idea? Make a clear argument on either yes or no. Write NO LESS than 60 words

I think making every piece of clothes more expensive cannot be the solution. Many low-income families can only afford clothes that are relatively cheap and thus depend on inexpensive clothes. In addition to that, making a shirt more expensive does not automatically mean that it is more sustainable. The price is only one component out of many. Finally, prices for private goods should not be determined by the government but by the basic principle of demand and supply.

Tipps & Tricks
Der erste Satz sollte in jedem Fall erst einmal die Haltung des Schreibenden ausdrücken. Im Anschluss kann man eine Vielzahl von Punkten aufführen für sowohl „für" und „gegen". Der/Die Schülerin sollte seine/ihre Position mit mindestens zwei Begründungen untermauern. Diese sollten wiederum nachvollziehbar und logisch sein, z.B. *Nobody likes high prices* wäre eine sehr schwache Begründung und würde hier zum Punktabzug führen.

2. Schulaufgabe aus dem Englischen

Name: ____________________________

Stoff: Unit 2-3

I. Listening Comprehension

(Text aus Lösung 2x vorlesen lassen oder Audio in Durchblicker.org hören)

Aborigines

Listen to the following text twice. Answer the questions afterwards

[1]breeding = Brut

Questions on the text

Answer the following questions. Sometimes more than one answer is correct. Be sure to tick all the correct answers but do not tick too many or you won't get the full points

1. Australia is ...
 ___ the smallest country in the world..
 ___ the smallest continent in the world.
 ___ 21 times smaller than Germany.
 ___ 21 times the size of Germany.
 ___ a city in England.

2. The Aborigines...
 ___ make up a majority of Australians.
 ___ were the first animals in Australia.
 ___ were the first humans in Australia.
 ___ do not exist anymore.
 ___ are a tourist attraction.

Statement	true	false	not in the text
Australia is a tourist attraction.	( )	( )	( )
Kangaroos, monkeys and koalas all live in Australia.	( )	( )	( )
Lake Eyre is 15 meters above sea level.	( )	( )	( )
The Aborigines came to Australia over 5.000 years ago.	( )	( )	( )
Sydney is a city in Australia.	( )	( )	( )
Lake Eyre is good for the breeding events for hens.	( )	( )	( )
Australia is a movie.	( )	( )	( )
Australia is bordering the Pacific Ocean.	( )	( )	( )
Australian English is easy to understand.	( )	( )	( )
Winter in Australia is from July until August.	( )	( )	( )

____/ 20

II. Vocabulary

1. Translate the following words from unit 2

1. Konsum / Verbrauch: ______________________

2. ökologisch: ______________________

3. nachhaltig: ________________________

4. Waschmittel / Reinigungsmittel: ____________________

5. schätzen: ___________________

6. angenehm, zweckmäßig: _______________________

7. vorhersagen: __________________

8. erbärmlich: ___________________

9. ekelhaft: ___________________

10. auspacken: ___________________

11. Erleichterung: ___________________

____/11

2. Fill in the gaps with vocabulary from unit 2 &3. Mind grammar and tenses where necessary

1. The __________________ of plastic has a negative effect on the environment.

2. FAQ is the abbreviation for "__________________ asked questions."

3. Air traffic ______________ many tons of carbon dioxide.

4. My battery is low. My smartphone needs to be ______________________.

5. It was a very ___________________ moment when my boyfriend asked me to marry him.

6. It is very _____________________ that the bus stop is right next to our hotel.

7. This restaurant not only offers „take away" but also ______________________.

8. Why do you favour _________________ over diesel?

9. Some employers ask for a letter of ____________________.

10. Many things that lay in the future are __________________________.

____/10

III. English Language Proficiency / Grammar

1. Change the following sentences into indirect speech

1. „Tanya is at home."
Mum said that ____

2. „Karim was ill."
David said that ____

3. „We have cleaned the house."

Sabine and Tanya told me that ____________________

4. „I didn't have time to do my chores."

Tanya told me that ____________________

5. „I am going to ride my bicycle."

David said that ____________________

6. „My brother flew to New York last year."

David told me that ____________________

7. „Tanya went to the supermarket an hour ago."

My mother said that ____________________

8. „My cousin will celebrate his graduation next weekend."

Karim told me that ____________________

9. „I spent all my money on Saturday."

Tanya said that ____________________

10. „Our professor will go to Munich tomorrow."

David told me that ____________________

____/20

2. Rewrite each sentence with a participle construction

1. The cars which are produced in Germany are nice.

____

2. I saw the woman. She came to the store.

____

3. When you go to Scotland you improve your English.

____

4. The car industry has come into the focus of environmental activists because it causes a lot of CO_2.

____

5. When it has been produced, the car is sent to the car dealer.

____

____/5

3. Answer the following questions with *So, Neither, Nor*

1. He is very good with students. (Ich auch/ebenso)

____

2. She plays the piano. (Mein Bruder auch/ebenso)

____

3. He has never been to New York. (Ich auch nicht)

____

4. I wouldn't mind helping you with your homework. (Er auch nicht)

____

5. I don't play video games. (Er auch nicht)

____

____/5

Total points ____/71

Good luck !

Lösung: 2. Schulaufgabe aus dem Englischen

I. Listening Comprehension *(Text 2x vorlesen lassen oder Audio in Durchblicker.org)*

Aborigines

Listen to the following text twice. Answer the questions afterwards

The first humans to live in Australia were the Aborigines. It is known that the first Aborigines immigrated to Australia over 50.000 years ago from Asia. Up to this day there are Aborigines living in Australia but it is rarely that a tourist can see them. They want to keep to themselves and do not want to be a tourist attraction.

Australia is the smallest continent but 21 times the size of Germany. The land is relatively flat. The seasons in Australia are the opposite from the northern hemisphere. Australia's summer is from December until February and their wintertime is from June to August. The North can have tropical temperatures and there is a rain season from November until April.

Even if one has great English skills, understanding Australians' will be a challenge. The Australian slang differs especially in the choice of words and pronunciation from British and American English. Therefore it is oftentimes hard to understand native Australians.

In Australia's forests you can find a lot of eucalyptus trees. Animals such as the kangaroo, koala or emu are what Australia is famous for. There are street signs announcing these animals.

Australia borders the Indian Ocean and the Pacific Ocean. Lake Eyre is Australia's lowest point at about 15 meters below sea level. It only rarely fills with water and usually has a number of sub lakes. In good years the lake can fill and if it does it is a great living area for birds. This is because it then supports major breeding[1] events of birds for example the Australian Pelican.

Questions on the text

Answer the following questions. Sometimes more than one answer is correct. Be sure to tick all the correct answers but do not tick too many or you won't get the full points.

1. Australia is …

___ the smallest country in the world.
_x_ the smallest continent in the world.
___ 21 times smaller than Germany.
_x_ 21 times the size of Germany.
___ a city in England.

2. The Aborigines...

___ make up a majority of Australians.
___ were the first animals in Australia.
_x_ were the first humans in Australia.
___ do not exist anymore.
___ are a tourist attraction.

Statement	**true**	**false**	**not in text**
Australia is a tourist attraction	( )	(x)	( )
Kangaroos, monkeys and koalas all live in Australia.	( )	(x)	( )
Lake Eyre is 15 meters above sea level.	( )	(x)	( )
The Aborigines came to Australia over 5.000 years ago.	( )	(x)	( )
Sydney is a city in Australia.	( )	( )	(x)
Lake Eyre is good for the breeding events for hens.	( )	(x)	( )
Australia is a movie.	( )	( )	(x)
Australia is bordering the Pacific Ocean.	(x)	( )	( )
Australian English is easy to understand.	( )	(x)	( )
Winter in Australia is from July until August.	( )	(x)	( )

II. Vocabulary

1. Translate the following words from unit 2

1. Konsum / Verbrauch: *consumption*
Tipps & Tricks: Verb: *to consume*
2. ökologisch: *ecological*
3. nachhaltig: *sustainable*
Tipps & Tricks: Gegenteil: *unsustainable*
4. Waschmittel / Reinigungsmittel: *detergent*
5. schätzen: *to estimate*
6. angenehm, zweckmäßig: *convenient*
7. vorhersagen: *to predict*
8. erbärmlich: *pathetic*
9. ekelhaft: *disgusting*
10. auspacken: *to unwrap*
Tipps & Tricks: Gegenteil: *to wrap*
11. Erleichterung: *relief*

2. Fill in the gaps with vocabulary from unit 2 &3. Mind grammar and tenses where necessary

1. The *disposal* of plastic has a negative effect on the environment.
2. FAQ is the abbreviation for "*frequently* asked questions."
3. Air traffic *emits* many tons of carbon dioxide.
4. My battery is low. My smartphone needs to be *charged.*
5. It was a very *emotional* moment when my boyfriend asked me to marry him.
6. It is very *convenient* that the bus stop is right next to our hotel.

Tipps & Tricks: Gegenteil → *inconvenient*

7. This restaurant not only offers "take away" but also *delivery.*
8. Why do you favour *petrol* over diesel?
9. Some employers ask for a letter of *reference.*
10. Many things that lay in the future are *unpredictable.*

Tipps & Tricks: Gegenteil → *predictable*

III. English Language Proficiency / Grammar

Change the following sentences into indirect speech

1. „Tanya is at home."
Mum said that *Tanya was at home.*
2. „Karim was ill."
David said that *Karim had been ill.*
3. „We have cleaned the house."
Sabine and Tanya told me that *they had cleaned the house.*
4. „I didn't have time to do my chores."
Tanya told me that *she hadn't had time to do her chores.*
5. „I am going to ride my bicycle."
David said that *he was going to ride his bicycle.*
6. „My brother flew to New York last year."
David told me that *his brother had flown to New York the year before.*
7. „Tanya went to the supermarket an hour ago."
My mother said that *Tanya had gone to the supermarket an hour before.*
8. „My cousin will celebrate his graduation next weekend."
Karim told me that *his cousin would celebrate his graduation the following weekend.*
9. „I spent all my money on Saturday."
Tanya said that *she had spent all her money on Saturday.*
10. „Our professor will go to Munich tomorrow."
David told me that *their professor would go to Munich the next day.*

Tipps & Tricks
Die **indirekte Rede** benutzt man zur Wiedergabe von Äußerungen.
Die Zeiten im Englischen verändern sich wie folgt:

Simple forms:	**Progressive forms:**
Simple present → Simple past	*am/are/is → was/were*
Simple past → Past perfect	*was/were → had been*
Present perfect → Past perfect	*has been → had been*
Past perfect → Past perfect	*had been → had been*
Future *will → would*	

Zeit- / Ortangaben verändern sich ebenso in der indirekten Rede.
this morning → that morning
today → that day
these days → those days
now → then
a month ago → a month before
last month → the month before / the previous month
next month → the following month
tomorrow → the next / following day
here → there

2. Rewrite each sentence with a participle construction

1. The cars which are produced in Germany are nice.
The cars produced in Germany are nice.
2. I saw the woman. She came to the store.
I saw the woman coming to the store.
3. When you go to Scotland you improve your English.
Going to Scotland improves your English.
4. The car industry has come into the focus of environmental activists because it causes a lot of CO_2.
Causing a lot of CO_2, the car industry has come into the focus of environmental activists.
5. When it has been produced, the car is sent to the car dealer.
Having been produced, the car is sent to the car dealer.

Tipps & Tricks
Partizipkonstruktionen werden in der Regel wie folgt benutzt:
- um Relativsätze zu kürzen
- um aus zwei Sätzen, einen Satz zu machen
- nach Verben der Wahrnehmung (z.B. sehen, sehen, hören, hören, riechen, fühlen)
- nach Verben von Ruhezustand und Bewegung (z.B. laufen, gehen, kommen, bleiben, stehen, liegen, sitzen)
- nach dem Verb „have“
- anstelle eines Nebensatzes

3. Answer the following questions with *So, Neither, Nor*

1. He is very good with students. (Ich auch/ebenso)
So am I.
2. She plays the piano. (Mein Bruder auch/ebenso)
So does my brother.
3. He has never been to New York. (Ich auch nicht)
Neither/Nor have I.
4. I wouldn't mind helping you with your homework. (Er auch nicht)
Neither/Nor would he.
5. I don't play video games. (Er auch nicht)
Neither/Nor does he.

Tipps & Tricks: *So* (positive Antwort), *Neither / Nor* (negative Antwort) werden oft in Antworten benutzt um diese zu betonen.

3. Schulaufgabe aus dem Englischen

Name: ________________________

Stoff: Unit 3

I. Reading Comprehension

Read the following text carefully and answer the questions below

Gender: Early Socialization[54]

Gender socialization is the process through which children learn about the social expectations, attitudes and behaviours typically associated with boys and girls. This topic looks at this socialization process and the factors that influence gender development in children

How important is it?

Gender socialization is the process through which children learn about the social expectations, attitudes and behaviours associated with one's gender. As children attain a sense of their own gender identity (i. e., knowing whether they are a girl or a boy), they pay heightened attention to information related to gender, and especially to same-gender models. This gender awareness, in combination with an early exposure to gender from multiple sources of socialization such as parents, siblings[55] and peers, has immediate consequences on children's attitudes and behaviours toward members of their own and other-gender group. For example, children may favour their own gender in their attitudes (having more positive feelings towards own-group members) and show gender discriminatory behaviours (preferring to interact with members of their own gender only). This gender segregation, may be supported by adults but more often is the choice of children themselves and may become problematic because children need to be able to function in gender-integrated settings[56] (e.g., day care or school). While children develop skills to interact with members of their own gender, their abilities to relate effectively with girls and boys are more limited. Accordingly, it is important to provide young children opportunities to play in mixed-gender groups in order to help them develop positive interpersonal relationships with both boys and girls across a range of settings.

What do we know?

Gender is one of the first social categories children become aware of. By the time they are three years old, they have formed their gender identity. They also begin to learn cultural gender stereotypes: that certain behaviours, activities, toys and interests are typical for boys and girls. Although children play an active role in shaping their gender identity development, their knowledge about gender comes from many sources of socialization, including parents, peers and teachers.

Parents

Parents provide children with their first lessons about gender. Although gender-egalitarian attitudes have increased in many cultures over the past decades, parents and especially fathers typically have different expectations for their sons and daughters with regard to personality

---

[54] socialization: Sozialisierung
[55] siblings: Geschwister
[56] gender-integrated settings: geschlechtsintegrierte Einstellungen

traits, abilities and activities. Parents' roles inside and outside the family also influence children's conception of gender roles. Nowadays, most women pursue jobs outside of the home, and men are increasingly involved in child care and housework. Interestingly, children who are raised by same-gender parents or who are exposed to father's child care involvement may be less likely to endorse[57] gender stereotypes. In addition, father's participation in domestic duties and/or child care is associated with a lower likelihood of violence[58] toward children. Finally, parents reinforce[59] gender stereotypes when they provide their sons and daughters with different toys, or when they describe general patterns about each gender (e.g., "girls like dolls while boys like football").

Peers
Another important way in which children learn about gender is through their interactions with peers. During early childhood, children prefer to play with peers who share similar interests or who they believe share those interests, and thus are more likely to be socialized by their same gender peers. While spending time with their friends, boys and girls learn what is appropriate for one gender or the other. This gender socialization can be direct or indirect. For example, children learn about gender stereotypes through their peers' direct comments (e.g., "long hair is for girls while short hair is for boys") and/or negative reactions when failing to conform to their gender expectations. Likewise, children learn and adopt gender-stereotypical behaviours (boy-typical versus girl-typical behaviours) as they spend more time interacting with members of their own gender.

Teachers / School
In addition to parents and peers, teachers are another source of gender socialization. Similar to parents, teachers have gender expectations, model gender roles, and reinforce gender-stereotypical behaviours in their classrooms. For example, educators may reinforce gender stereotypes by labelling and organizing students in group activities or by creating different activity centres for boys and girls. This gender segregation, in turn highlights gender as a social category and reinforces children's gender stereotypes and avoidance of cross-gender playmates[60].
Although it is clear that parents, peers and teachers socialize children to think and act in gendered ways, boys' and girls' development is also influenced by biological factors, such as sex hormones, which influences children's preferences for activities. As such, gender's development might be best described as resulting from the interaction between gender socialization and biological factors.

What can be done?
Parents and service providers are encouraged to provide children with a wide range of toys and activities during early childhood. Likewise, it is recommended that parents and teachers create playful environments where children interact positively with both boys and girls. These interactions would help children to develop skills to interact effectively in mixed-gender groups and to gain a better understanding of gender differences and similarities. In fact, parents, educators and practitioners are highly encouraged to pay attention to the stereotypic

---
[57] to endorse: billigen, befürworten
[58] a lower likelihood of violence: eine geringe Wahrscheinlichkeit von Gewaltanwendung
[59] to reinforce: verstärken
[60] avoidance of cross-gender playmates: Vermeidung von geschlechtsübergreifenden Spielkameraden

beliefs children express regarding each gender, as some may foster[61] negative behaviours and attitudes against the other gender. This concern can be addressed by exposing children to counter-stereotypic models (e.g., a female hockey player or a male nurse) and by teaching them that being a girl or boy is more than just looking pretty or acting tough. Indeed, it is recommended that parents and educators discuss and challenge gender stereotypes with children (e.g., 'girls can also be great soccer players'). Yet, while it is recommended to challenge children's gender stereotypes, interventions might be most effective when they make gender less salient as opposed to more salient[62]. Finally, educational policy makers are encouraged to emphasize the importance of co-educational school environments as they promote more gender-egalitarian attitudes and behaviours than all-boys/girls schools.

[This text has been taken from Encyclopedia On Early Childhood Development; Accessed: 20 June 2021: https://www.child-encyclopedia.com/gender-early-socialization/synthesis]

Decide which of the following statements is true (T), false (F) or not in the text (NT)

1. Learning about the social expectations from others is a part of the gender socialization process.

O T O F O NT

2. Children are already exposed to gender norms at an early age.

O T O F O NT

3. Friends are not a source of socialization.

O T O F O NT

4. Some children only engage with other children of the same gender.

O T O F O NT

5. Only adults are responsible for gender segregation.

O T O F O NT

6. Gender segregation helps children to function in school.

O T O F O NT

7. Girls are generally able to relate effectively to both boys as well as other girls.

O T O F O NT

8. Children already form their gender identity when they are very young.

O T O F O NT

9. Playing with toy dinosaurs is typical for boys.

O T O F O NT

10. Children often learn their first lessons about gender from their mother and father.

O T O F O NT

---

[61] as some may foster: wie manche es fördern mögen

[62] less salient as opposed to more salient: weniger hervorstechend im Gegensatz zu mehr hervorstechend

11. Every father is nowadays involved in child care and housework.

O T O F O NT

12. Children from gay couples are less likely to endorse gender stereotypes.

O T O F O NT

13. Parents should not buy their children gender-typical toys.

O T O F O NT

14. Gender socialization is not always direct.

O T O F O NT

15. Boys learn many gender-stereotypical behaviours when they spend time with girls.

O T O F O NT

16. Teachers play a lesser role in gender socialization than parents.

O T O F O NT

17. The development of someone's gender is only influenced by socialization.

O T O F O NT

18. During early childhood, parents should buy their children more toys.

O T O F O NT

19. Gender-stereotypes cannot be eliminated in the future.

O T O F O NT

20. Policy makers can also help overcome gender-stereotypes.

O T O F O NT

____/20

II. Vocabulary

Fill in the gaps with words from unit 3

1. I don't need the latest iPhone or the coolest pair of sneakers. I am not ________________.

2. He doesn't have a boss; he works as a ________________ consultant.

3. ____________________ how rich you are, I won't go on a date with you.

4. When you apply for a job here, you will need a ________________________ from your former boss.

5. Studying six hours of English every day is very ________________________.

6. Many people don't ________________________ climate change.

7. He was ________________ to hear that his parcel had arrived.

8. Tanya spent four years studying for her business degree. _________________, she continued to work at her father's company.

9. Her parents are _________________ her studies so she won't have to work.

10. They have torn down the ____________________ building.

____/10

III. English Language Proficiency / Grammar

Put the following words in the correct order to form a sentence. Pay attention to punctuation

1. painting /. / which / door /, / red / My / a / needs / house /, / has (2 P)

2. The / he / old / is / yesterday / car /, / months / which / five /bought /. / , (2 P)

3. The / bad /. / that / was / job / really / first / got / I (2 P)

4. at /, /, /. / had / about / to / Tanya / first job / a / popular cinema / whose / wishes / she / boss / more money / was / spoken / her (4 P)

____/10

IV. Translation

Translate the following excerpt from the reading comprehension above into German

"What do we know?
Gender is one of the first social categories children become aware of. By the time they are three years old, they have formed their gender identity. They also begin to learn cultural gender stereotypes: that certain behaviours, activities, toys and interests are typical for boys and girls. Although children play an active role in shaping their gender identity development, their knowledge about gender comes from many sources of socialization, including parents, peers and teachers." Use an extra sheet

____/10

Total points ____/50

Good luck !

Lösung: 3. Schulaufgabe aus dem Englischen

I. Reading Comprehension

Read the text "Gender: Early Socialization" carefully and answer the questions below Decide which of the following statements is true (T), false (F) or not in the text (NT)

1. Learning about the social expectations from others is a part of the gender socialization process.

✔ T ○ F ○ NT

2. Children are already exposed to gender norms at an early age.

✔ T ○ F ○ NT

3. Friends are not a source of socialization.

○ T ✔ F ○ NT

Tipps & Tricks: Im Text ist die Rede von *peers*, worunter Freunde in diesem Kontext fallen.

4. Some children only engage with other children of the same gender.

✔ T ○ F ○ NT

5. Only adults are responsible for gender segregation.

○ T ✔ F ○ NT

Tipps & Tricks: Zwar sind Erwachsene auch verantwortlich, aber die Kinder selber ebenso.

6. Gender segregation helps children to function in school.

○ T ✔ F ○ NT

7. Girls generally relate effectively to both boys as well as other girls.

○ T ✔ F ○ NT

Tipps & Tricks: Im Text ist die Rede vom gleichen Geschlecht, was bei Mädchen also andere Mädchen wären.

8. Children already form their gender identity when they are very young.

✔ T ○ F ○ NT

Tipps & Tricks: Ab dem Alter von etwa 3 Jahren.

9. Playing with toy dinosaurs is typical for boys.

○ T ○ F ✔ NT

Tipps & Tricks: Dies mag vielleicht so sein, steht aber nicht im Text.

10. Children often learn their first lessons about gender from their mother and father.

✔T ○ F ○ NT

Tipps & Tricks: Da im Text die Rede von *parents* ist, stimmt diese Aussage.

11. Every father is nowadays involved in child care and housework.

○ T ✔F ○ NT

Tipps & Tricks: Im Text wird lediglich erwähnt, dass mehr und mehr Väter dies tun, aber eben nicht alle.

12. Children from gay couples are less likely to endorse gender stereotypes.

✔T ○ F ○ NT

13. Parents should not buy their children gender-typical toys.

○ T ○ F ✔ NT

Tipps & Tricks: Dies wäre vielleicht wünschenswert, wird aber nicht explizit vorgeschlagen.

14. Gender socialization is not always direct.

✔T ○ F ○ NT

Tipps & Tricks: Sondern ebenso indirekt.

15. Boys learn many gender-stereotypical behaviours when they spend time with girls.

○ T ✔F ○ NT

Tipps & Tricks: Wenn sie viel Zeit mit anderen Jungen verbringen, das Gegenteil ist also der Fall.

16. Teachers play a lesser role in gender socialization than parents.

○ T ○ F ✔NT

Tipps & Tricks: Mag vielleicht so sein, wird im Text aber nicht erwähnt.

17. The development of someone's gender is only influenced by socialization.

○ T ✔F ○ NT

Tipps & Tricks: Biologische Faktoren spielen ebenso eine Rolle.

18. During early childhood, parents should buy their children more toys.

○ T ○ F ✔NT

Tipps & Tricks: Im Text ist lediglich die Rede davon, den Kindern eine größere Auswahl (and verschiedensten Spielsachen) zu bieten. Dies impliziert aber nicht, dass Kindern generell mehr Spielzeug gekauft werden soll.

19. Gender-stereotypes cannot be eliminated in the future.

○ T ○ F ✔ NT

Tipps & Tricks: Womöglich nicht, dies steht aber nicht im Text.

20. Policy makers can also help overcome gender-stereotypes.

✔T ○ F ○ NT

II. Vocabulary

Fill in the gaps with words from unit 3

1. I don't need the latest iPhone or the coolest pair of sneakers. I am not *materialistic.*
2. He doesn't have a boss; he works as a *freelance* consultant.
3. *No matter* how rich you are, I won't go on a date with you.
4. When you apply for a job here, you will need a *reference* from your former boss.
5. Studying six hours of English every day is very *exhausting.*
6. Many people don't *acknowledge* climate change.
7. He was *pleased* to hear that his parcel had arrived.
8. Tanya spent four years studying for her business degree. *Meanwhile,* she continued to work at her father's company.
9. Her parents are *funding* her studies so she won't have to work.
10. They have torn down the *entire* building.

III. English Language Proficiency / Grammar

Put the following words in the correct order to form a sentence. Pay attention to punctuation

1. painting /. / which / door /, / red / My / a / needs / house /, / has

My house, which has a red door, needs painting.

2. The / he / old / is / yesterday / car /, / months / which / five /bought /. / ,

The car, which he bought yesterday, is five months old.

3. The / bad /. / that / was / job / really / first / got / I

The first job that I got was really bad.

4. at / , / , / . / had / about / to / Tanya / first job / a / popular cinema / whose / wishes / she / boss / more money / was / spoken / her

Tanya, whose first job was at a popular cinema, wishes she had spoken to her boss about more money.

Tipps & Tricks
1. **Definitionsklauseln** (restriktive Klauseln) → KEINE KOMMAS
Ein definierender (restriktiver) Satz ist ein Satz, der für den Sinn des Satzes wesentlich ist.
Beispiel: My house *that has a red door* needs painting.
Hier ist die rote Tür ein charakteristisches Merkmal. Sie hilft, dieses Haus von anderen Häusern zu unterscheiden.
2. **Nicht definierende Klauseln** (nicht einschränkende Klauseln) → KOMMAS
Eine nicht definierende (nicht einschränkende) Klausel kann als in Klammern betrachtet werden.
Beispiel: My house, *which has a red door*, needs painting.
Die kursiven Wörter sind praktisch eine Nebensache und könnten weggelassen werden. Der eigentliche Punkt des Satzes ist, dass das Haus gestrichen werden muss; die rote Tür ist nebensächlich.

IV. Translation

Translate the following excerpt from the reading comprehension above into German

"What do we know?
Gender is one of the first social categories children become aware of. By the time they are three years old, they have formed their gender identity. They also begin to learn cultural gender stereotypes: that certain behaviours, activities, toys and interests are typical for boys and girls. Although children play an active role in shaping their gender identity development, their knowledge about gender comes from many sources of socialization, including parents, peers and teachers."

Was wissen wir?
„Gender" (beziehungsweise das soziale Geschlecht) ist eine der ersten sozialen Kategorien, die Kindern bewusst werden. Wenn sie drei Jahre alt sind / Mit drei Jahren haben sie ihre Geschlechtsidentität (bereits) gebildet / geformt. Sie beginnen auch, kulturelle Geschlechter-stereotypen zu erlernen: dass (zum Beispiel) bestimmte Verhaltensweisen, Aktivitäten, Spielzeuge und Interessen typisch für Jungen und Mädchen sind. Obwohl Kinder eine aktive Rolle bei der Entwicklung ihrer Geschlechtsidentität spielen, entspringt / kommt ihr Wissen über „Gender" aus vielen Quellen der Sozialisation / Sozialisierung, einschließlich Eltern, Gleichaltrigen und Lehrern.

Tipps & Tricks
Gender darf als mittlerweile eingedeutschtes Wort übernommen werden (muss aber nicht).
Die oben benutzen Schrägstriche und -klammern sollen nur aufzeigen, dass es viele Möglichkeiten gibt, diesen Text korrekt zu übersetzen.

3. Schulaufgabe aus dem Englischen

Name: ______________________________

Stoff: Unit 3

I. Listening Comprehension *(Text aus Lösung 2x vorlesen lassen oder Audio in Durchblicker.org hören)*

Ten steps to a successful CV (curriculum vitae)

Listen to a text about how to write a CV (curriculum vitae). You will hear the text twice. Do not panic if there is a word you do not know / understand. Just keep listening and focus on the questions at hand. Make sure you read through all statements and questions before the audio starts

Writing a good CV can be one of the toughest challenges of job hunting. Most employers spend just a few seconds scanning each CV before sticking it in the ‚Yes' or ‚No' pile

Vocabulary you might not know

CV – Lebenslauf; pile – Stapel; a sure-fire way – eine todsichere Methode; punchy – schlagkräftig; niggly – niedlich; whizzed – zischte, gezischt; job advert – Stellenanzeige; cynical bunch – zynischer Haufen; spin – Rolle, Nebeneffekt, Interpretation; head of recruitment and resourcing – Leiter der Personalbeschaffung; to dismiss – entlassen, abweisen; blatant lies – unverfrorene Lügen; awkward – peinlich; dull – stumpf, langweilig; to upload – hochladen; recruiters – Personalvermittler; buzzwords – Schlagwörter; to input – eingeben

a) Decide which of the following statements is true (T), false (F) or not in the text (NT)

1. A CV should normally be no longer than 2 pages.

O **T** O **F** O **NT**

2. Recruiters do not spend a lot of time on each single CV.

O **T** O **F** O **NT**

3. The same CV should be sent to lots of employers.

O **T** O **F** O **NT**

4. You also have to send a personal statement to your potential employer.

O **T** O **F** O **NT**

5. Having been out of work always looks bad on your CV.

O **T** O **F** O **NT**

6. You're CV doesn't have to be updated regularly.

O **T** O **F** O **NT**

7. Small errors in your CV are okay.

O **T** O **F** O **NT**

8. Using numbers on your CV can potentially help your application.

O **T** O **F** O **NT**

9. The most creative applicants usually get the job interview.

O T O F O NT

10. Keywords on your CV are key.

O T O F O NT

b) Answer each question *briefly* (sometimes one or two words are enough)

1. How much time do employers / recruiters spend on each CV on average?

____

2. What should you do before applying to a job at a specific company?

____

3. What is the personal statement for?

____

4. What should you avoid on your CV if you have been out of work?

____

5. Is it necessary to keep your CV up-to-date even when you are not looking for a job?

____

6. Apart from finding out whether you are a suitable candidate, what do employers also look for on your CV?

____

7. How do employers sometimes find out whether a candidate has been lying on his CV?

____

8. What else can you do to make your CV stand out?

____

9. How can employers find you?

____

10. What should you use if you want to find out which (key)words are often used in conjunction with your desired job?

____

____/20

II. English Language Proficiency / Grammar

Stressing sentence parts: Alan is planning a holiday in the USA. He's at a travel agency. Answer the questions in full sentences. Use five different ways of stressing the answers

1. The travel agent: Do you need a train ticket?

Alan: No, ____

2. The travel agent: I don't think you have a credit card?

Alan: ____

3. The travel agent: Did your mother give you her credit card?

Alan: ____

4. The travel agent: Do you sometimes have money problems abroad?

Alan: ____

5. The travel agent: You must be pleased to be going on holiday soon.

Alan: ____

____/10

III. Text Production

Write a short cover letter / personal statement for the internship advertisement below. Apply what you have learned in unit 3. As this job ad is fictional, you may invent skills (or past work experience) but make sure your statement fits the proposed position. Write NO LESS than 150 words

21.08.2021

Our tutoring institute "Effective Learning" is looking for a new intern for teaching English to 5th graders as a second language. If you enjoy teaching English to beginners, you are welcome to apply for this position.

Necessary requirements:
- excellent English and German language skills
- be a student of a German "Gymnasium" and be at least in 9th grade
- excellent communication skills, and good command of Microsoft Office (incl. PowerPoint)
- strong teamwork skills
- highly motivated

Desirable:
- previous relevant work experience

Please address your complete application to Mr Mustermann and let us know your earliest start date.

Effective Learning
Hauptstraße 10
80331 München

____/20

Total points ____/50

Good luck !

Lösung: 3. Schulaufgabe aus dem Englischen

I. Listening Comprehension *(Text 2x vorlesen lassen oder Audio in Durchblicker.org hören)*

Ten steps to a successful CV (curriculum vitae)

Listen to this text about how to write a CV (curriculum vitae). You will hear the text twice. Do not panic if there is a word you do not know / understand. Just keep listening and focus on the questions at hand. Make sure you read through all statements and questions before the audio starts

Writing a good CV can be one of the toughest challenges of job hunting. Most employers spend just a few seconds scanning each CV before sticking it in the ‚Yes' or ‚No' pile. Here are the top 10 tips for writing a CV that'll secure the all-important interview

1. Keep it real! [short pause]

Usually, a CV should be no more than two pages – and that's two pages of A4 paper! Employers spend, an average, just 8 seconds looking at any one CV, and a sure-fire way of landing yourself on the no pile is to send them your entire life story. Keep it punchy, to the point, and save those niggly little details for the interview.

2. Tailor it [short pause]

We've all done it. Whizzed the same CV out to lots of employers to save time… Stop! Take the time to change your CV for each role that you apply for. Research the company and use the job advert to work out EXACTLY what skills you should point out to them. They will appreciate the obvious effort.

3. Include a personal statement [short pause]

Don't just assume an employer will see how your experience relates to their job. Instead, use a short personal statement to explain why you are the best person for the job. This should be reflected in your cover letter as well see our tips to the perfect cover letter.

4. Don't leave gaps [short pause]

We are a cynical bunch and leaving obvious gaps on your CV immediately makes employers suspicious – and they won't give you the benefit of the doubt. If you've been out of work it can be a worry but just put a positive spin on it. Did you do a course, volunteer work or develop soft skills such as communication, teamwork or project management? If so, shout about it!

5. Keep it current [short pause]

You should keep your CV up-to-date whether you're looking for a job or not. Every time something significant occurs in your career, record it so you don't later forget something that could be important.

6. The error of your ways [short pause]

Employers ***do*** look for mistakes on CVs and if they find them, it makes you look really bad. David Hipkin, head of recruitment and resourcing at Reed Business Information, warns, 'With most employers experiencing massive volumes of applicants right now, giving them the excuse to dismiss your application because of avoidable errors is not going to help you secure an interview.' If you're unsure then use a spellchecker and ask someone else to double-check what you've written. And don't ignore the most common CV mistakes.

7. Tell the truth [short pause]
Everyone lies on their CV, right? ***No!*** Stop! Blatant lies on your CV can land you in a whole heap of trouble when it comes to employers checking your background and references. The last thing you want is to start work and then lose your new job for lying. You also may get caught out at the interview stage when you suddenly can't answer questions on what you claim to know. And that can be ***very*** awkward!

8. The maths [short pause]
This may sound dull but by backing up your achievements with numbers it makes selling yourself much easier. When writing your work history, don't just say that you increased sales; tell them you increased sales by 70% over a six-month period. Get it? Big numbers are especially good (although don't forget point 7 of our list!).

9. Make it look good [short pause]
We live in a world where image is everything, and that also goes for your CV. Take some time to pretty it up… Use bullet points and keep sentences short. Use the graphic design trick of leaving plenty of white space around text and between categories to make the layout easy on the eye. Alternatively, get creative with your job application!

10. Make it keyword friendly [short pause]
If you've uploaded your CV to a job site so recruiters can find you, keywords are very important. Job titles and job buzzwords will help a search engine pick out your CV from the pile. Confused? Don't be. A marketing candidate might mention SEO (Search Engine Optimization), direct marketing and digital marketing among their experience and skills, for example… If you're not sure, have a search online and see what words are commonly mentioned when you input your job title.

[This text has been taken from totaljobs.com; it has been slightly altered to suit this exercise; Accessed: 20 June 2021: https://www.totaljobs.com/advice/successful-cv]

a) Decide which of the following statements is true (T), false (F) or not in the text (NT)

1. A CV should normally be no longer than 2 pages.

✔ **T** ○ **F** ○ **NT**

2. Recruiters do not spend a lot of time on each single CV.

✔ **T** ○ **F** ○ **NT**

Tipps & Tricks: Gerade mal 8 Sekunden.

3. The same CV should be sent to lots of employers.

○ **T** ✔ **F** ○ **NT**

Tipps & Tricks: Jeder CV sollte auf die jeweilige Stelle / Firma zugeschnitten sein.

4. You also have to send a personal statement to your potential employer.

✔ **T** ○ **F** ○ **NT**

5. Having been out of work always looks bad on your CV.

○ T ✔ F ○ NT

Tipps & Tricks: Nicht wenn man weiß, wie man diese Lücke geschickt füllt, somit stimmt diese verallgemeinernde Aussage nicht.

6. You're CV doesn't have to be updated regularly.

○ T ✔ F ○ NT

7. Small errors in your CV are okay.

○ T ✔ F ○ NT

Tipps & Tricks: Selbst kleinste Fehler können zum Ausschluss führen.

8. Using numbers on your CV can potentially help your application.

✔ T ○ F ○ NT

9. The most creative applicants usually get the job interview.

○ T ○ F ✔ NT

Tipps & Tricks: Sicherlich ist es hilfreich kreativ zu sein, allerdings wird im Text keine Aussage darüber getroffen, ob Kreative normalerweise die Nase vorn haben.

10. Keywords on your CV are key.

✔ T ○ F ○ NT

b) Answer each question *briefly* (sometimes one or two words are enough)

1. How much time do employers/recruiters spend on each CV on average?
Eight/8 seconds.
2. What should you do before applying to a job at a specific company?
Research the company / Inform yourself about the company.
3. What is the personal statement for?
To explain why you are the best / suitable person for the job.
4. What should you avoid on your CV if you have been out of work?
Leaving gaps
5. Is it necessary to keep your CV up-to-date even when you are not looking for a job?
Yes
6. Apart from finding out whether you are a suitable candidate, what do employers also look for on your CV?
Mistakes / Errors
7. How do employers sometimes find out whether a candidate has been lying on his CV?
Through checking the candidate's background and references.
8. What else can you do to make your CV stand out?
Make it look good / Prettying it up / Good graphic design
9. How can employers find you?
When you upload your CV online / keywords online.

10. What should you use if you want to find out which (key)words are often used in conjunction with your desired job?
Search online

II. English Language Proficiency / Grammar

Stressing sentence parts: Alan is planning a holiday in the USA. He's at a travel agency. Answer the questions in full sentences. Use five different ways of stressing the answers

1. The travel agent: Do you need a train ticket?
Alan: *No, what I need is a plane ticket.*
2. The travel agent: I don't think you have a credit card?
Alan: *I do have a credit card.*
3. The travel agent: Did your mother give you her credit card?
Alan: *It was my father who gave me his credit card.*
4. The travel agent: Do you sometimes have money problems abroad?
Alan: *I'm always having money problems abroad.*
5. The travel agent: You must be pleased to be going on holiday soon.
Alan: *I'm really pleased to be going on holiday soon.*

Tipps & Tricks
Hervorhebungen von Satzteilen kannst du auf verschiedene Weise machen:
1. Hervorhebung mit *do*: Du kannst hiermit **spontan Gefühle ausdrücken** oder eine **Aufforderung** unterstreichen, außerdem kannst du jemandem widersprechen.
2. Hervorhebung mit *it is / it was*: Mit *it is / it was* kannst du jeden Satzteil (außer Verb) hervorheben.
3. Hervorhebung mit ***what*-Sätzen**: mit *what* + eine Form von *be* kannst du Satzteile hervorheben.
4. Du kannst auch das ***Present progressive*** zum Hervorheben von Verwunderung und Verärgerung benützen. (Zusätzlich zum ***Present progressive*** kannst du noch das Adverb *always* verwenden.)
5. Mit **Adverbien** kannst du auch Dinge / Handlungen hervorheben. Einige Beispiele sind *really, absolutely, very, often, quite, completely, even terribly...*

III. Text Production

Write a short cover letter / personal statement for the internship advertisement below. Apply what you have learned in unit 3. As this job ad is fictional, you may invent skills (or past work experience) but make sure your statement fits the proposed position (s.S. 67). Write NO LESS than 150 words

Effective Learning
Max Mustermann
Hauptstraße 10
80331 München

Erika Ehrlich
Bahnhofstraße 1
80337 München *20.08.2021*

Dear Mr Mustermann,
I was very glad to read that you are currently looking for a new intern at your institute. In the following, I would like to briefly introduce myself and demonstrate why I am the best candidate for your advertised position.
My name is Erika Ehrlich, and I am a current 9th-grade student at the XXX Gymnasium in Munich. Since I started learning English as a second language in school, I have always received an A or B in all of my exams proving, that my English is sufficient to teach 5th graders. Since this school year, I am also a voluntary tutor at our school helping 5th graders with their English homework in the afternoon. This helped me to improve my teamwork and communication skills with students at that age. Finally, having given numerous presentations at my own school, I also have good knowledge of Microsoft PowerPoint.
You will be hiring a confident, reliable, and highly motivated intern. As I am currently working on another assignment, my earliest start date would be 1st August 2021. I am sure I will make a great addition to "Effective Learning" and I am looking forward to hearing from you.
Sincerely,
Erika Ehrlich

Tipps & Tricks
Folgendes sollte unbedingt beachtet werden:
1. Ein **korrekter Briefkopf** gehört unbedingt in ein Anschreiben (auch Datum sollte nicht vergessen werden).
2. Das Anschreiben muss (wie gefordert) an den **Recruiter** gerichtet sein.
3. Auf alle in der Anzeige erwähnten Punkte sollte eingegangen werden. Es reicht NICHT lediglich zu sagen, dass man z.B. gut in Englisch ist. Man sollte diesbezüglich Beispiele / Beweise aufführen.
4. Umgangssprache unbedingt vermeiden.
5. Korrekte FORMALE Grußformel am Ende. → Auch möglich: *Kind regards; Respectfully; Faithfully; Cordially;* etc.

Monika und Claus Arndt aus Waldtrudering geben im Eigenverlag Lernhilfen für Schüler heraus

Die Durchblick-Garanten

Die Tage sind gezählt bis zu den Sommerferien. Nicht alle Schüler jedoch tun sechs Wochen lang nichts für die Schule. Und es gibt so einige Eltern, die sich jetzt schon fürs neue Schuljahr rüsten. Viele von ihnen landen bei Monika und Claus Arndt aus Waldtrudering. Das Ehepaar gibt Hefte mit Schulproben für Grundschüler und Schulaufgaben für Gymnasiasten und Realschüler heraus. Kinder und Jugendliche können sich mit ihren Durchblicker-Aufgaben auf Prüfungen vorbereiten.

Monika und Claus Arndt im Keller ihres Waldtruderinger Hauses. Dort drucken sie ihre Durchblicker-Schulaufgaben. Jahrelang haben sie zudem Nachhilfeunterricht gegeben, mittlerweile konzentrieren sie sich auf ihr Verlagsgeschäft. Ihre Schulaufgaben sind im Buchhandel zu finden und helfen Schülern bei der Lösung von Schulaufgaben. *Fotos: Panthermedia/ve/kn*

Im Keller der Familie Arndt im Birkhahnweg in Waldtrudering läuft der Drucker. In den Regalen stapeln sich ordentlich die Ausdrucke. Ihre Bestellungen erreichen Monika und Claus Arndt meist spät abends. Nach Ladenschluss schicken Buchhändler noch ihre Bestellliste ab, so auch an den Durchblicker Verlag in Waldtrudering. Viele Jahre lang haben die Arndts im Keller Schülern Nachhilfeunterricht gegeben. Vor fünf Jahren haben sie einen Verlag gegründet und verkaufen seitdem Bücher mit typischen Schulaufgaben für bayerische Schüler. Derzeit, kurz vor den Sommerferien und vor allem dann im September, sei die Nachfrage besonders groß. „Wir haben ein saisonales Geschäft", sagt Claus Arndt schmunzelnd. Bevor es in die Ferien geht oder zum Start ins neue Schuljahr, bestellen Schüler und ihre Eltern die Durchblicker-Schulaufgaben.

Der Mathematiker sattelte aufs Lehramt um

Die Arndts haben sozusagen eine Marktlücke entdeckt: Verlage bieten zwar immer mehr Lernhilfen für Schüler an. Doch die Arndts haben ihre Ausgaben auf die jeweiligen Schultypen und auf die neuen Lehrpläne in Bayern zugeschnitten. So läuft und läuft ihr Drucker. „Volltreffer!", hat ihnen ein Schüler geschrieben, „drei Aufgaben in meiner Schulaufgabe waren genau wie die aus Ihrem Buch!" Und eine Buchhändlerin lässt sie wissen: „Ich empfehle die Reihe immer weiter. Sie haben in mir einen Fan gefunden."

Wie aber kommt es, dass die beiden Waldtruderinger so einen guten Riecher haben, wie Lehrer ihre Schulaufgaben gestalten und was sie wollen? Claus Arndt war als Diplom-Mathematiker in der EDV-Branche beschäftigt. Bis 2004. Da hieß es: „Wer gehen wolle, könne gehen." Der Waldtruderinger Vater zweier Söhne ließ sich das nicht zwei Mal sagen. Händeringend wurde damals nach Lehrern gesucht. So sattelte der Mathematiker kurzerhand um und unterrichtete fortan an der Realschule in Dachau und am Neuperlacher Heinrich-Heine-Gymnasium Mathe.

Damit nicht genug. Zuhause im Keller eröffnete er mit seiner Frau Monika ein Lernstudio für Schüler. Claus Arndt gab Nachhilfe in Mathematik. Seine Frau in Englisch, Deutsch und Französisch. „Für Physik und Latein beschäftigten wir noch weitere Nachhilfelehrer", erzählt Claus Arndt. Die Waldtruderinger Familien nahmen das Angebot gerne an: Bei den Arndts gab es Nachhilfe für den Achtklässler, der darum kämpfte, wegen Mathe bloß nicht durchzufallen. Ein anderer Bub, ein Grundschüler, konnte partout nicht stillsitzen. „Ich ließ ihn hier unten auf einem kleinen Trampolin auf- und abspringen und fragte ihn dabei das Einmaleins ab", erzählt Claus Arndt. Ebenso ackerten gleich mehrere Schüler in einem Crashkurs, um in ihrer Abschlussprüfung eine bessere Note zu bekommen.

Nachhilfeunterricht von 13 bis 20 Uhr

Vier Jahre lang büffelten die Nachhilfelehrer mit ihren Schützlingen Stunde für Stunde im Keller. „Unseren Höhepunkt hatten wir im Jahr 2008, da saßen wir von 13 bis 20 Uhr in unserem Lernstudio, die Nachfrage in Waldtrudering und Umgebung war einfach so groß", erinnert sich Claus Arndt. Was ist das Arndtsche Erfolgsrezept? Die Arndts lösen mit ihren Schülern Schulaufgaben, erarbeiten Musterlösungen und korrigieren die Antworten gemeinsam. „Diese Klassenarbeiten denken wir uns selbst aus", sagt Claus Arndt. Im Laufe der Jahre haben sie ein Gespür dafür entwickelt, welche Aufgabentypen drankommen können — „wie die Lehrer ticken".

Schulaufgaben zu entwickeln, das machte Claus Arndt bald nicht nur für seine Nachhilfeschüler im Münchner Osten. Für die Verlage Klett und Cornelsen modifizierte er Schulaufgaben. „Doch die Lehrpläne variieren von Bundesland zu Bundesland", erzählt der Klausuren-Profi. Und so schlug man ihm vor, für Bayern einfach selbst Schulaufgaben herauszugeben. Im Eigenverlag.

Claus Arndt hatte ja mit seiner Frau Monika kompetente Hilfe an seiner Seite. Denn vor allem sie war es, die in ganz Bayern Buchhändler abklapperte, um Werbung für die Durchblicker-Schulaufgaben zu machen. Mehr noch: Monika Arndt hatte als Autorin bereits Ernährungsbücher für Kinder veröffentlicht, hatte unter anderem beim Stark-Verlag über Produktion sowie Inhalt von Lernhilfen viele Erfahrungen gesammelt und als Lektorin gearbeitet. Sie knöpfte sich nun die Fächer Deutsch, Französisch und Englisch vor und arbeitete ebenso Schulaufgaben aus. Zudem sei es für sie als Schulaufgaben-Entwickler mit Einführung des G8 leichter geworden: „Alles ist systematischer und strukturierter, ich kann eher abschätzen, was in einer Klassenarbeit drankommt", sagt Claus Arndt.

Neu im Angebot sind Proben für Grundschüler

Mittlerweile haben sie eine breite Palette mit 57 verschiedenen Ausgaben im Angebot: Ob für Gymnasiasten Mathe-Schulaufgaben von der fünften bis hoch zur zwölften Klasse oder für Realschüler Englisch-Schulaufgaben. „Und neu und sehr beliebt sind unsere Schulproben in Mathe, Deutsch und HSU für Dritt- und Viertklässler", sagt Monika Arndt. „Die sind immer mehr unsere Renner!" Als Verlag profitieren sie von dem wachsendem Druck, der schon auf Grundschüler ausgeübt werde. „Eltern wollen unbedingt, dass ihr Kind einen Notendurchschnitt von 2,33 beim Übertrittszeugnis in der vierten Klasse hat, damit es aufs Gymnasium gehen kann", sagt Claus Arndt. „Das ist oft zu viel des Guten." Er weiß, wovon er spricht. Er hat in all den Jahren in seinem Lernstudio viele Kinder kennengelernt. „Oft haben wir gemerkt, welch großen Druck Eltern auf ihr Kind ausüben können." Natürlich müsse sich jedes Kind auf Tests in der Schule vorbereiten. Doch als Eltern zweier Söhne, 1993 und 1996 geboren, wissen sie eben auch, dass ein Kind nicht zu viel lernen dürfe. „Wer für eine Schulaufgabe mit zwei unserer Aufgaben übt, dem reicht das meist", behauptet Monika Arndt.

Den beiden Schulaufgaben- und Nachhilfe-Profis geht es vor allem darum, Schüler besser auf das vorzubereiten, was sie bei einer Probe erwartet. „Angst und Nervosität legen sich schnell, wenn Schüler ähnliche Aufgaben kennen und bereits bearbeitet haben", sagt Claus Arndt.

Verena Rudolf

Telefon (089) 53 06-420
lokales@merkur.de
Telefax: (089) 53 06-86 56

Münchner Merkur Nr. 285 | Freitag, 9. Dezember 2016

Mehr Durchblick für Schüler

Claus und Monika Arndt produzieren Lernhefte im heimischen Keller in Waldtrudering

VON LAURA MÜLLER

Vielen Kindern graut es vor der Schule. Häufig sind sie unmotiviert und wissen nicht, wie sie sich auf Tests und Schularbeiten vorbereiten sollen. Für diese Problematik gibt es eine Menge Nachhilfelehrer und Bücher, die helfen sollen. Einer der Verlage, die solche Bücher, oder vielmehr Hefte, produzieren, ist der Durchblicker Verlag – ein kleiner Buchverlag, der nur aus dem Ehepaar Claus und Monika Arndt besteht. Er hat sich auf Schulaufgaben und ihre Lösungen spezialisiert. Die Arndts produzieren die Hefte im heimischen Keller in Waldtrudering.

Auf den jungen Schülern lastet eine Menge Druck, sagen die Arndts

Claus Arndt, ein ehemaliger Software-Ingenieur, hat den Verlag vor fünf Jahren gegründet. Angefangen hat alles damit, dass Claus Arndt anfing, Nachhilfe zu geben. „Als die Kinder kamen, wollte ich nicht ständig unterwegs sein", erzählte er. „Also habe ich meinen Job gekündigt und Nachhilfe gegeben." Die Schüler kamen gerne zu Claus Arndt, so wurde die Nachfrage irgendwann zu groß. Die Arndts gaben das Lernbüro auf und fingen an, Bücher mit Schulaufgaben und ihren Lösungen zu drucken. Zunächst verkauften sie nur wenige Hefte, doch im vergangenen Jahr waren es schon 20 000. Insgesamt haben sie 58 Bücher verfasst und herausgebracht. Die Arndts sehen sich mittlerweile als „ernst zu nehmende Konkurrenz" für den renommierten Stark-Verlag. Dessen rote Übungsbücher stehen bei vielen Schülern im Regal.

Claus Arndt sammelt seit der Umstellung auf das G8 Schulaufgaben von verschiedenen Schulen. Weil er selbst mal als Lehrer arbeitete, weiß er, was andere Lehrer erwarten. Claus und Monika Arndt orientieren sich bei ihren Aufgaben immer an dem neusten Stand der Lehrpläne.

Als die Arndts ihren Verlag gründeten, klapperten sie alle möglichen Büchereien ab, um ihre Bücher präsentieren zu können. Monika Arndt hat schon vorher als Lektorin und Autorin gearbeitet. Sie kennt sich in der Branche aus und weiß, wie man hier etwas erreicht. Heute liegen die Bücher des Durchblicker-Verlags etwa in Hugendubel- und Thalia-Filialen aus. „Wir freuen uns, dass unsere Bücher so gut ankommen", sagt Claus Arndt. Am besten verkaufen sich laut den Arndts die Lerntrainer für die Grundschule sowie für die 5. und 6. Klasse Gymnasium. Das verwundert. Claus Arndt erklärt: „Auf den jungen Schülern lastet schon eine Menge Druck."

Die Nachfrage ist groß: Im Keller von Monika und Claus Arndt stapeln sich die Lernhefte des heimischen Verlags. Alles ist handproduziert, das ist das Markenzeichen des Verlags.

FOTOS: ASTRID SCHMIDHUBER

Die Hefte des Durchblicker-Verlags: Insgesamt 58 Lerntrainer haben die Arndts schon herausgebracht.

Am besten verkaufen sich die Lerntrainer für Grundschule und 5. und 6. Klasse

Als die Arndts die Bücher in immer größerer Stückzahl verkauften, stellte sich die Frage, wie sie die Lerntrainer weiter produzieren wollen. Sie entschieden sich, die Bücher selbst zu drucken. „Alles ist handproduziert, das ist unser Markenzeichen", sagt Monika Arndt.

Sie legen Wert darauf, dass ihre Aufgaben schulnah sind und so auch wirklich abgefragt werden könnten. „Außerdem ist es wichtig für uns, die Schüler für das Lernen zu motivieren. Häufig schreiben Kinder schlechte Noten, weil sie zu wenig Selbstvertrauen haben", sagt Claus Arndt. „Wenn die Kinder mit unseren Schultrainern lernen, erkennen sie Aufgaben aus dem Unterricht wieder, das gibt ihnen ein Erfolgserlebnis und motiviert sie." Natürlich könnten die Bücher keine schon vorher entstandenen Wissenslücken schließen, „aber sie helfen, zu vertiefen und zu wiederholen."

AKTUELLES IN KÜRZE

38-Jähriger stirbt nach Drogenkonsum

Ein 38-jähriger Münchner ist am vergangenen Freitag an den Folgen von Kokain- und Alkoholkonsum gestorben. Nach Angaben der Polizei wurde der arbeitslose Münchner am Donnerstag, 17. November, in eine Klinik eingeliefert. Dort musste er reanimiert werden. In seinem Urin wurde ein hoher Kokaingehalt festgestellt. Zudem hatte er eine Alkoholvergiftung. Die Obduktion ergab, dass der 38-Jährige an einer Überdosis Rauschgift gestorben war. Die Polizei schließt Fremdverschulden aus. plm

Rechte und Pflichten von Mietern

Viele Auseinandersetzungen zwischen Vermietern und Mietern resultieren daraus, dass die Parteien ihre Rechte und Pflichten nicht kennen oder diese falsch einschätzen. Die Rechtsanwältin Gisela Weber vom Mieterverein München erläutert bei einem Infoabend im Bauzentrum München, Willy-Brandt-Allee 10, am Dienstag, 13. Dezember, ab 18 Uhr, welche Klauseln Mieter vor der Unterzeichnung eines Formularmietvertrages besonders unter die Lupe nehmen sollten. Sie spricht außerdem die Probleme des Alltags an, die im täglichen Umgang zwischen den Mietvertragsparteien und den Nachbarn auftreten können. Der Eintritt ist frei. do